T0318910

Cambridge Elements =

Elements in Ethics
edited by
Ben Eggleston
University of Kansas
Dale E. Miller
Old Dominion University, Virginia

MORAL RELATIVISM
AND PLURALISM

David B. Wong
Duke University

Shaftesbury Road, Cambridge CB2 8EA, United Kingdom

One Liberty Plaza, 20th Floor, New York, NY 10006, USA

477 Williamstown Road, Port Melbourne, VIC 3207, Australia

314–321, 3rd Floor, Plot 3, Splendor Forum, Jasola District Centre,
New Delhi – 110025, India

103 Penang Road, #05–06/07, Visioncrest Commercial, Singapore 238467

Cambridge University Press is part of Cambridge University Press & Assessment,
a department of the University of Cambridge.

We share the University's mission to contribute to society through the pursuit of
education, learning and research at the highest international levels of excellence.

www.cambridge.org
Information on this title: www.cambridge.org/9781009044301

DOI: 10.1017/9781009043496

First published 2023

A catalogue record for this publication is available from the British Library.

ISBN 978-1-009-04430-1 Paperback
ISSN 2516-4031 (online)
ISSN 2516-4023 (print)

Moral Relativism and Pluralism

Elements in Ethics

DOI: 10.1017/9781009043496
First published online: January 2023

David B. Wong
Duke University

Author for correspondence: David B. Wong, dbwong@duke.edu

Abstract: The argument for metaethical relativism, the view that there is no single true or most justified morality, is that it is part of the best explanation of the most difficult moral disagreements. The argument for this view features a comparison between traditions that highly value relationship and community and traditions that highly value personal autonomy of the individual and rights. It is held that moralities are best understood as emerging from human culture in response to the need to promote and regulate interpersonal cooperation and internal motivational coherence in the individual. The argument ends in the conclusion that there is a bounded plurality of true and most justified moralities that accomplish these functions. The normative implications of this form of metaethical relativism are explored, with specific focus on female genital cutting and abortion.

Keywords: moral relativism, ethical theory, comparative philosophy, normative ethics, naturalistic ethics

ISBNs: 9781009044301 (PB), 9781009043496 (OC)
ISSNs: 2516-4031 (online), 2516-4023 (print)

Contents

Contents

1 Why Are People So Exercised about Moral Relativism?

Growing up Chinese American in the American Midwest, the ways of my family, including what was expected of me as a son, seemed painfully different from the ways of the families of my European American friends. Family seemed so much more important in my home. This did not mean that my European American friends had no responsibilities to their families, but in general, their duties rested upon their shoulders more lightly. My mother once said to me that she simply didn't understand (maybe she meant didn't approve of) the American obsession with happiness. She thought the most important thing was to fulfill one's responsibilities to others, and of course the weightiest ones were owed to family. I don't think she meant to deny the importance of a subjective sense of contentment (what I think she meant by "happiness"), but her point was that the subjective sense had to be earned through the performance of responsibilities, as best as one could. I respected her sentiments, and half of me agreed with her, but the other half wanted to be free to pursue happiness.

The question was about how I should live my life, and so it took on the greatest personal importance for me. When I began to take moral relativism seriously, some of those closest to me wondered whether I should find some other philosophical subject to write about. Many people think that moral relativism licenses any answer a person would be inclined to give, or any answer their society's culture gives. That is why "moral relativism" is often used as an epithet, a term of derision by people who assume that morality is a matter for reasoned judgment. I agree with this assumption, but depart from the oft-associated, but very different one that for any moral question there is a single correct answer to be found and that conflicting answers are incorrect. Others, and I am among them, have come to question the latter assumption by reflecting on the nature of moral disagreement. The kinds of disagreement that can be most effectively adduced in support of moral relativism typically involve values that come into conflict, each of which are compelling in their own right (consider liberty versus equality). The experience of moral conflict can be interpersonal, in which different sides have different views as to which value is most compelling given the circumstances. Conflict also can be intrapersonal. That is, one can be internally divided between two moral viewpoints, as was the case for me after my discussion with my mother.

The mere fact that people disagree, intrapersonally or interpersonally, is not in itself a reason to think that there isn't a single correct answer to be found. Insufficient evidence to resolve a disagreement is compatible with there being a single correct answer. The interpretive frameworks that people bring to assessing the evidence can differ markedly, producing conflicting views, but this too is compatible with there being a single correct answer. The motivation that people have for adopting beliefs, moral and otherwise, and whether they are aware of their motivation or not, is often that these beliefs are held by others with whom they identify or align themselves. Beliefs can help people protect their self-esteem, and this can lead to motivations to overlook evidence that undermines these beliefs and focus on evidence that supports them. Take the belief that people are solely responsible for what they have achieved in life, which plays a key role in certain conservative views about distributive justice. If one has enjoyed reasonable success, one may strongly believe that one did so on one's own, focusing on the genuinely difficult situations one had to work one's way through, but not so much keeping in mind the help others provided along the way. This is a very familiar way of coming to an ill-founded belief, and philosophers point to such epistemic pitfalls to argue that moral disagreement provides little or no evidence against metaethical universalism (e.g., see Brink 1989). But one can agree that such pitfalls exist, and still reject the idea that they "explain away" all important moral disagreement.

In what follows, I make a case for this rejection and for accepting some versions of moral relativism. The path begins with a discussion of how to frame the issue of moral relativism. What exactly are the views being debated for which certain kinds of moral disagreements are adduced as evidence?

2 How Should Theses about Moral Relativism Be Framed?

In philosophy, so much depends on how you frame the question. The best way of framing the question enables interlocutors to fully consider the main considerations that have motivated the contending sides, and to evaluate the full array of possible conclusions that could be justified by those considerations. A less-desirable framing would narrow the range of motivating considerations or the possible conclusions that could be reached. With this in mind, "metaethical moral relativism" is defined here as the thesis that there is no single true or most justified morality (with some adaptation, this formulation is from Harman 2000, 77). Morality here is taken as a guide to what sort of actions and attitudes are required, prohibited, and permissible, and much of its subject matter concerns how one is to relate to and affect others, though it can also specify for the individual what it is to live a worthwhile life. The disjunction, "true or most justified," is meant to allow for the possible position that morality is not the sort of thing that is true or false (as an order or admonition might not be true or false), but nevertheless can be justified, perhaps in greater or lesser degree (as an order or admonition might be more or less well taken). Relativism, thus defined, is opposed to what I shall call "universalism": the view that there is a single true or most justified morality.

This view is sometimes called "absolutism," which seems the natural opposing term for "relativism," but I will use "universalism" since the other term is often used to refer to another type of normative view that there are moral prescriptive truths that hold without exceptions, such as "Never lie."

The type of moral relativism thus defined is "metaethical" as opposed to "normative" moral relativism. The metaethical thesis does not purport to tell us what is morally right or wrong or what a morally good life is. Normative moral relativism is the subject of Sections 17–24, but we will have occasion to address some normative questions about what we ought to do throughout this Element. Metaethics addresses metaphysical and epistemological issues that often arise when we confront puzzles and difficulties in trying to answer the first-order normative questions about what to do or how to live. In particular, puzzling about the – sometimes seemingly intractable – moral differences between people and even within the belief system of a single person can lead to belief in metaethical relativism.

Metaethical moral relativism, as defined here, embraces a capacious set of possibilities. It contrasts with more specific definitions that are usually more extreme: for example, the view that the truth or justifiability of a morality is determined by whatever standards or practices are established within a group or even by a single person. This is metaethical relativism as "anything goes." While the definition proffered here includes the extreme version as a possibility, it also includes what one might call a moderate form of relativism or a strong form of pluralism: the view that more than one morality is true or most justified but that not all moralities are true or most justified. It will be argued in Sections 3–16 that this latter view is most consistent with the best explanation of both similarities and differences in moral belief and practice, with empirically grounded theories of the major roles they play in human life, and with recent empirical evidence as to laypeople's attitudes toward moral objectivity.

3 Relationship and Community, Autonomy and Rights

Many people have experienced the kind of conflict I experienced. Some of them are immigrants or the children of immigrants (as I am), to a developed country. One way of describing the conflict in a general way is to say that it obtains between duties arising from relationship and membership in community, on the one hand, and on the other hand, rights to personal autonomy that provide a protected space to live as one pleases. The film *A Great Wall* (1986) depicts an interpersonal conflict of values occasioned by a Chinese American family's trip to China to visit the father's sister and her family. The daughter from the Chinese family learns the concept of privacy from the son of the Chinese

American family, and deploys the concept in objecting to her mother's opening and reading her mail before handing it to her. The mother reacts to her daughter's indignation with bafflement: Why should she need permission to learn what is going on for her daughter?

These value conflicts come under the more general heading of relationship and community, on the one hand, and on the other hand, autonomy and individual rights. For example, the right to freedom of speech can come into conflict with the value of promoting and protecting relationships of mutual concern and trust. A case can be made for restricting speech when it seriously threatens basic forms of shared understanding that form part of the framework of mutual trust. Not only can this framework be undermined through speech that intimidates and foments hatred, but it can turn the value of speech against itself through causing those it victimizes to be silenced for fear of identifying themselves as members of the targeted group (consider the brutal psychological terrorism often waged over social media these days). Sometimes historical events tilt the weight of judgment in favor of restriction – see, for example, the illegality of Holocaust denial in many European countries – and sometimes acts of intimidation are so egregious that they clearly merit the punishment of law, as in the case of the students at the University of Mississippi who both hung a noose and draped the Confederate battle flag around the statue of James Meredith, the university's first black student (Srvluga 2015). Even if in such cases it is fairly clear what should be done, there are many cases in which it is not. It is important to recognize that the values on each side of the conflicts mentioned can be in relationships of mutual support as well as discord. The absence of relations of mutual caring and respect has historically in the United States led to the willingness to prevent disfavored groups – for example women, African Americans, Native or First Americans, and those coming or descended from people from Asian countries (depending on the historical period and the country of origin) – from being accorded equal status or citizenship, or from being able to exercise their rights to vote and assemble for political participation. Supporting the value of relationship can support the rights of those with whom one is in relationship.

There is comparatively little attention paid to conflict between relationship and autonomy in academic moral philosophy, at least when compared with conflict between the value of acting for the greatest good of the greatest number and the rights of individuals to have their most compelling interests protected, even if sacrificing those interests is for the greater good. The dominance of the argumentative dialectic around the latter conflict in modern Western moral philosophy explains this disparity of attention. The fact that so much of the oxygen is consumed by the dialectic is itself revealing of an assumption shared by the opposing sides: that the individual is taken as morally basic, whether it be the welfare or happiness or utility of the individual, which under one of the most dominant forms of consequentialism is to be aggregated and maximized, or some trait individuals possess, such as rationality or the possession of basic interests, in virtue of which they have rights. By contrast, moral conflicts of the first kind involve at least one side taking relationship as a foremost value. Moralities that emphasize the value of relationship in prominent ways are found all over the world, and are at least as pervasive as moralities emphasizing rights or promotion of utility. Conflicts involving the value of relationship with the other two kinds of value need not involve one side denying that the other side's values are values at all. Indeed, it need not involve denying that the other side's values are important. It can involve a difference in the value priorities of the different sides.

As implied by my first example derived from personal experience, there are cultural differences in these value priorities. Cultures in which relationship is given high priority include not just the ones expressed by Chinese Confucian ethics, but Ubuntu ethics associated with South Africa, Zimbabwe, and Malawi. There are Indigenous ethics, such as those of many Native American peoples, for example the Ojibwe, Chippewa, and Anishanaabe. Not only do these ethics generally have in common the high priority they place on having relationships of the right sort (e.g., both Confucian and Ubuntu ethics stress that being a realized person is to be in relationship with other persons; see Metz 2011), but the relational ethic can in some of its forms acknowledge the organic interdependence of all life and is extended toward parts of the environment that go beyond the human: plants, animals, and the land and water. These parts are sometimes conceived and treated in ways similar to one's human kin (Coulthard 2014; Whyte 2018; Murdock 2020; Hourdequin 2021). To return to the Chinese tradition, Daoism emphasizes the human relationship to the rest of nature and points to what can be learned from the operation of natural processes that contrast with the rigidity and fixedness of conventional human conceptualizations of the way things work (Hourdequin and Wong 2005).

Within contemporary Western moral philosophy, Alasdair MacIntyre (1988, 2007), Michael Sandel (1998), and Charles Taylor (1985, 1989) have presented distinctive and sophisticated critiques of consequentialist and deontological normative theories. It is not within the project of this Element to discuss their theories, but it is sufficient to point out here that their preferred normative theories each give prominent place to an ethic of relationship and community. There are significant differences between these three thinkers in the extent and manner in which they believe the values of relationship can be made compatible with ethics that emphasize rights and autonomy. Those working in care ethics present a similar alternative, at least on a very general level, to consequentialist and deontological normative theories. Uniting the diverse work of thinkers such as Annette Baier (1986), Carol Gilligan (1982), Virginia Held (2006), Eva Kittay (1999), Nel Noddings (1984), Sara Ruddick (1989), Joan Tronto (1993), and Margaret Urban Walker (2007) is accordance of greater priority to the value of relationships and the recognition that this emphasis on relationship poses a significant alternative to the two dominant traditions of modern Western moral philosophy. Though the care ethic is strongly associated with feminist ethics, Chenyang Li (1994) has drawn attention to the parallels between the care ethic and the Confucian ethic, which is the philosophical crystallization of the cultural tradition my mother was rooted in. There are a great many differences between Confucian and care ethics, as Li would acknowledge, but he is also right to point out that they share an important point of difference from the dominant mainstream of modern Western moral philosophy.

When taken together, these conflicts involving relationship and community on the one hand, and (personal) autonomy and individual rights on the other hand indicate that there is a central issue that occurs repeatedly in normative moral thought and practice. That it does so says something about the complexity of what human beings value and what they need. The reader may still be unconvinced that there is need to delve further into this conflict. To take an example that is likely not to be purely hypothetical, some people among the likely audience for this Element may take the position that it is sufficient to dismiss relationship-centered moralities simply because they can come into conflict with rights-centered moralities. These people might take that position because they are so firm on the absolute correctness of there being certain rights that should not be violated. The next section argues that there are both epistemic and ethical reasons to delve further by addressing barriers to proper understanding of relationship-centered moralities on the part of those who subscribe to rights-centered moralities.

4 Epistemic Reasons to Delve Further into the Conflict between Relationship-Centered and Rights-Centered Moralities

Recent literature on the proper epistemic response to disagreement with another person is focused on situations in which the other is one's epistemic "peer." Factors that go into assessing peerhood include whether the parties are roughly equal in the relevant cognitive abilities they bring to the issue in dispute; whether there is unequal bias on the issue; and whether they have the same evidence. The question is then raised as to whether peer disagreement with another gives one reason to think one is mistaken in holding one's own position.

A typical example features friends, after dinner at a restaurant, calculating how much of a tip each should leave the server. They agree to divide equally a tip of twenty percent of the total bill, and do the math in their heads, but they end up with different amounts. One well-known position on this kind of example is that the disagreement of one's peer gives one as much reason to doubt the correctness of one's answer as one has to stick with one's answer (Christensen 2007).

There are a variety of other positions on the correct epistemic stance to take, but the point to be made here is that the moral disagreements just discussed raise a rather different question: whether one has sufficient information to make a reasonable judgment as to whether the parties to the disagreement *are* peers. Do the opposing sides have the same evidence? While ordinary facts, such as how much the total bill is, can certainly count as part of the evidence in moral disagreements over what is right and wrong, such facts get taken into account from the standpoint of perspectives composed of configurations of values. The opposing sides have perspectives that significantly differ from each other, even when there is considerable overlap in the values. Given that people arrive at their positions in a disagreement on the basis of their value perspectives, we should know with some specificity what those perspectives are and what evidence they have for adopting them. In the peer disagreement literature, one option for appropriate epistemic response to the restaurant tip case is suspending belief as to what is the correct amount. In the sort of cases of moral disagreement under discussion here, the appropriate response is further sustained and concerted inquiry. This is in fact the uptake of Christensen's influential article on the import of disagreement for the activity of knowledge seeking: that in many cases we should take moral disagreement as the opportunity to improve on our knowledge (Christensen 2007).

Given the practical urgency of acting on *moral* belief in particular, suspension of belief may not be a morally viable option. As will be discussed in Sections 18–20, declining epistemic confidence in the justifiability of one's moral beliefs may appropriately affect *how* one acts on them. The immediate point at this stage in the argument, however, is that further inquiry is required as a matter of epistemic rationality. While it is possible to simply stand unmoved on the basis of one's strong moral intuitions (such as intuitions about what rights people have and the scope of those rights as they collide with other moral considerations), one should know that others have had similarly unshakable intuitions very different from one's own. Within the nonmoral realm, there seem to be few intuitions people tended to have about the geometrical properties of physical space that seemed as unshakable as the axioms that set up Euclidean geometry (e.g., that the shortest distance between two points is a straight line and that there is only one line going through a point not on another line and that is parallel to that other line). Yet current mathematics regards these axioms not as necessary truths about physical space but as hypotheses to which there are alternatives. Alternative geometries have physical application and are part of a revolution in how space is scientifically conceived. We would do well to test our current intuitions against the intuitions that have driven other value perspectives. As a practical matter, we may have to act on our values at any given time, but that does not prevent us from conducting inquiry into the moral traditions of others.

We do not know how our epistemic situations compare to those of others who hold these other value perspectives. To the extent that one has not seriously investigated other traditions, and also veins of thought and practice within what could broadly be deemed one's own tradition (think of care ethics and defenses of more relationally oriented ethics within the modern Western tradition), one should have one's confidence dented in the singular truth or justifiability of one's own value perspective. The various ways that one can misjudge, accept stereotypes, and simply not make enough of an effort to understand heighten the epistemic challenge. Studies reveal tendencies to exaggerate the similarities among members of a group and to be biased in favor of our own groups and denigrate other groups (see Tajfel 1970; Tajfel et al. 1971; Tajfel and Turner 1979). We should take such results as a caution about our tendency to make quick judgments about the immorality of others.

The epistemic argument I have just made is intended to be a universal argument addressed to the question of what is the epistemically rational response to the types of moral disagreement mentioned. Given the normative importance of knowing how others decide on and morally justify their ways of acting, we should conduct inquiry into the traditions that ground their decisions as a matter of thoroughness and conscientiousness. Further, knowing that our evaluations of others tend to be biased and provincial, we should try to correct course through exercising our curiosity. To be clear, pressing one's inquiry into the reasons that others might have for their moral positions is not in itself an argument for metaethical moral relativism. It could just as well result in the conclusion of metaethical universalism. The point is that both those disposed toward relativism and toward universalism should be looking into the most difficult and challenging moral disagreements to see if a single correct answer looks like it might eventually emerge. The metaethical moral relativist is prepared to argue that a single correct answer does not emerge and that we have little reason to think that one will.

Philosophers who are unsympathetic to metaethical moral relativism sometimes look down on the motivations of its proponents. The motivations purportedly show a kind of intellectual laziness, an unwillingness to try "to get to the bottom of things."[1] I don't deny that this is sometimes the kind of motivation to be found behind the view. At its best, however, moral relativism is motivated precisely by the desire to get to the bottom of things. From this point of view, it is the universalist who stops inquiry too soon, who is too ready to fall back on what seems self-evident and clear to them, at a point when they could inquire further into how other people have thought differently in ways that challenge that stopping point. In this guise, relativism is motivated by a sense of humility before the wide and variegated expanse of human experience and aspiration (in fact, the claim here is that it is rational to feel this sense of humility), and by a desire to learn from others, including those in different historical eras and different societies, those strange neighbors down the street, and difficult Aunt Julia across the table at the big family gathering. Far from being motivated by intellectual laziness, it is spurred by a willingness to challenge one's own deepest assumptions by discovering the different assumptions that others make. It is fed by the desire to discover not only what one's own best arguments for one's moral commitments are, but to discover what the best arguments of others are for their moral commitments. It rests on the resolve to balance as best as one can such motivations against the importance of standing for one's sense of what is right and just and good.

5 An Ethical Argument for Extended Inquiry into Rivals to One's Own Ethical Views

There is another, separate, and additional argument to be made for extended inquiry into the best arguments of others, and it in fact appeals to one's own sense of what is right and just and good. Because inquiry is an activity and therefore practical in itself and also in many of its ramifications for further action, it is subject to moral evaluation and prescription. In her work on epistemic injustice, Miranda Fricker has observed that "epistemology as it has traditionally been pursued has been impoverished by the lack of any theoretical framework conducive to revealing the ethical and political aspects of our epistemic conduct," and similarly, she observes, it is "equally a pity that ethics has not traditionally taken our epistemic conduct into its remit" (Fricker 2007, 2).

Here, we take up Fricker's appeal by pointing out that in mischaracterizing, simplifying, and stereotyping other people's moral traditions, we not only demonstrate a lack of respect for them but may also replicate beliefs that have served as rationalizations of our society's exploitation and oppression of these others.

---

[1] This phrase and the idea behind it as applied to relativism is taken from an interview of this author by Richard Marshall, online: www.3-16am.co.uk/articles/the-pluralist, accessed November 27, 2022.

Even if we do not ourselves personally or intentionally engage in such rationalization, we may be the unwitting inheritors of casual dismissals of the traditions of others, and risk burying what was done in the past and its ramifications into the present. Furthermore, as argued later in this section, we may have personally benefited from past misdeeds. I want to make clear that in presenting a normative argument for consistent and concerted inquiry into the moral traditions of others, I do not presume that the ethical premises upon which it rests are universally true for everyone. I ask only that the reader reflect on whether the argument holds force for them. I suspect that for a great many readers, it does, or should have, given my sense of what their values are.

Consider that many in the societies containing potential readers of this Element and others like it have benefited (intentionally or not, knowingly or not) from the exploitation and oppression of many of these others, in the past and present. This claim is addressed to those likely to be subscribed to moral traditions in which it is now recognized that it was quite wrong to have exploited and oppressed members of other societies, many of which contained moral traditions that prioritize relationships. Exploitation and oppression were justified by characterizing the civilizations of these people, including their moral traditions, as savage, barbaric, and inferior. Some of these characterizations could be determined in short order as plainly false and blatant rationalizations to which relatively few currently subscribe, but others are stereotypes that continue to be accepted by people who are widely thought to be far better informed and fair-minded, and this may frequently be the case, which doesn't mean they can't be wrong.

Into the first category of the plainly false and blatantly rationalizing falls an 1859 speech by a proslavery lawyer by the name of O'Connor who claims that

> to that condition of bondage the Negro is assigned by Nature. . . . He has the strength, and he has the power to labour; but the Nature which created that power has denied him either the intellect to govern or the willingness to work. . . . And that Nature which denied him the will to labour gave him a master to coerce that will, and to make him a useful servant in the clime in which he was capable of living useful for himself and for the master who governs him. (Millett 2007, 178)

Paul Millett remarks that this is a thoroughly Aristotelian defense of slavery, which in the modern context is applied to the races (Millett 2007, 178). Aristotle asserts that there are natural slaves suited by nature to be the possession of others and to be their instruments of action (Aristotle 2016, *Politics* 1.1, 1254a7–18). The soul is by nature the ruler of the body, and the intellect rules the appetites. Analogously, the male naturally rules over the female (1254a34–1254b15). And the use of slaves and tame animals is not very different, he says, because both minister to the needs of life with their bodies (1254b24–5). It is quite possible that this claim for the naturalness of enslaving some people answers, perhaps unconsciously, to Aristotle's perception that a well-lived life for some, including himself, depended on the slavery of others. As Heath observes, "Without natural slaves, the masters' natural capacity for *eudaimonia* would be frustrated; and nature does nothing in vain" (*Pol.* 1.9, 1256b20–1; Heath 2008, 264). That is, "enslaving people who were not natural slaves would be unjust, creating an internal contradiction even more fundamentally subversive of the good life" (Heath 2008, 264).

Much of the United States was built from the ancestral lands of Indigenous peoples, who were removed by force, and often in violations of treaties made with them, removed again from where they were sent when the land was desired in the westward expansion of the nation. President Andrew Jackson expressed the moral rationalization for these acts in his 1833 speech to Congress: "They have neither the intelligence, the industry, the moral habits, nor the desire of improvement which are essential to any favorable change in their condition. Established in the midst of another and a superior race, and without appreciating the causes of their inferiority or seeking to control them, they must necessarily yield to the force of circumstances and ere long disappear" (Richardson 2004). This stance toward Indigenous peoples took another form in the nineteenth- and twentieth-century practice, appearing in the United States and Canada, of taking Indigenous children away from their families and placing them in boarding schools with the express intent of wiping away their language and culture (Adams 1995; Morel 1997; Hanson et al. 2020).

As for Chinese Americans, I remember the family elders sitting in our living room and discussing bitterly the lynching and murders of Chinese in California. One editorial in a San Francisco newspaper called the Chinese "morally a far worse class" than black people and described them as "cunning and deceitful" and "libidinous and offensive" (Chang 2003). To this day, such characterizations have a familiar ring to many Chinese Americans. The Chinese Exclusion Act of 1882 was the first act to prohibit an ethnic working group from entry into the United States on the grounds that it endangered good order. Mexican Americans were also subject to lynching in California and parts of the Southwest. Though some were granted citizenship and land because they had lived and worked in territory taken by the United States in the Mexican-American War, their holdings were often taken illegally and sometimes by force, and their citizenship did not enable their rightful reclamation of the land. Like the Chinese, they often had no other viable option but to work in the lowest-paying jobs under terrible working conditions.

From these egregious acts, some in American society reaped benefits, which continue to be inherited by their descendants. One example is the university from which I received my PhD, Princeton, where scholars and student researchers have found that the man who deeded the land on which the university sits was a slave owner. The first nine presidents of the university were all at some point in their lives slave owners (Hollander and Sandelweiss 2022). Duke University, at which I am a professor, "rented" the labor of slaves when it was Trinity College (Gillespie 2020). The fact that I have been the indirect beneficiary of exploitation and oppression and am also a member of a group that has been exploited and oppressed is not unusual. Wrongdoing is infectious. I do not suggest that these contrasting statuses cancel each other out and result in a clean slate, so to speak. The fact that some Chinese Americans have been the subject of racist injustice does not mean that they cannot themselves be the perpetrators of such injustice toward members of other groups. Rather, it is incumbent on each one of us to identify how we might have benefited from injustice or to its compounding through perpetuating the mischaracterization of those who have suffered from it. And we have to appropriately respond to it even as we continue to insist on the rectification of injustice toward our own groups.

In the second category, which includes those with a much stronger claim to be better informed and fair-minded, are those who reject self-serving mythologies of race and gender. However, not all mistakes are as obvious as they seem with the benefit of time and cultural change. While one might dismiss the racist and sexist beliefs of earlier generations of Americans, one might still mischaracterize and stereotype others who seem to be different or live differently, and to do so in a way that compounds, however inadvertently, the egregious sort of exploitation and oppression practiced on these others. The ethical upshot of the recognition of one's own possible continuing contribution to compounded injustice is to examine one's own understanding of who these others are and how they seek to live. If one has drawn from one's own moral tradition to condemn the egregious injustice done to others, one should also interrogate the ideas one has of them, their values, and ways of life. Getting the wrong idea on these matters may lead to further injustice against them. We may have ideas of how to rectify past injustices done to them that they would reject or to which they would propose better alternatives. Our mistaken ideas about them, including what they value, may encourage wrongly paternalistic or condescending attitudes toward them. To reiterate, this is not a direct argument for metaethical relativism. Delving into the reasons of those on the opposing side of a moral disagreement may or may not result in greater appreciation for the force of those reasons, much less the conclusion that one has no persuasive case to overrule those reasons. All I have argued for so far is a particular way of trying to arrive at a decision between relativism and universalism, which is to pursue the arguments and reasons on both sides of the relevant disagreement and to see how we assess the force of reasons after such inquiry (the inquiry may be ongoing, so we may have to make provisional assessments).

In the next section, I proceed to give a sample of what such an investigation could look like. I will focus much of my attention on Confucian relational ethics, but will relate it to other types of relational ethics when the comparison seems apt. Keep in mind, however, that ethics that fall under the broad rubric of "relational" can be quite different from each other on greater levels of specificity and that there can be conflict among them on important matters.

6 Overcoming Stereotypes of Relationship-Centered Moralities

Those who subscribe to rights-centered moralities often dismiss relationship-centered moralities on the basis of stereotypes, for example, that such moralities subordinate or absorb the individual to or into the group. Social scientists often contribute to this stereotype, perhaps inadvertently, by labeling them as "collectivist" in orientation (e.g., Triandis 1995). The stereotype also includes the presence of strong and rigid social hierarchies: the father or the head of the family, the patriarch of the clan, tribal chief, and king. The stereotype may hold that "collectivist" moralities may have once served a good social function, perhaps under conditions that necessitated close cooperation between members of a group, but that development and new forms of technology have made such intensive forms of interdependence and hierarchy unnecessary.

It might further be said that those who remain wedded to relationship-centered ways of life may not have had experience of other more liberating and self-directed ways. Or they may benefit from being at or near the top of hierarchies that are endorsed under these moralities, and self-interest has biased their moral beliefs toward these moralities. Now, however, it might be said, the enlightened are in a position to clearly recognize the inherent dignity and worth of the individual and that such worth grounds rights that require for the individual opportunities and liberties to be protected against the demands of others and groups.

Recently, the stereotype has undergone some undermining. Some empirical studies of cultures in which relationship-centered values are prevalent have stressed not that the individual is subordinated to the group but that the person is conceived as an "interdependent" in contrast to an "independent" self (Markus and Kitayama 1991). Under the interdependent conception, one's identity as a person, and one's characteristic behavior and attitudes, are understood as responses to particular people in particular contexts. The kind of person one is depends on who one is with. The "independent" self is conceived as a free-standing individual with an identity that is detachable from the particular people one is interacting with. The interdependent conception has normative implications for what constitutes the good of the individual and how that good relates to the good of others. In accordance with the way one's identity can depend on whom one stands in relationship with, one's good *as an individual* depends on the goods of others. One has a compelling personal interest in their welfare and in one's relationship with them. Sustainable and morally viable relationships depend on the individuals' gaining satisfaction and fulfillment from being in those relationships. Rather than the individual's good being subordinated to others, the individual's good overlaps with the good of others. For example, the good of each member of a family may include or overlap with the good of other members of the family. When one family member flourishes, so do the others.

This is not to deny that some interpretations of relational ethics within their home traditions have sometimes fallen more on the collectivist, subordinating side. Moral traditions usually give rise to an array of alternative interpretations of their central values and how these values are to be prioritized in relation to one another. This of course is no less true of rights- or utility-centered traditions, but those working within those traditions take this variety of interpretations for granted, and especially if they are advocates of these traditions, are used to the task of discerning what they judge to be the best interpretation(s), one(s) that they judge to provide the most authentic and most plausible version(s). However, in interpreting other traditions (and much of the time "interpretation" is too generous a description), there is too often a very casual, unreflective assumption that the tradition is monolithic with respect to its content and practices. And little care is taken to examine the interpretations adopted.

In philosophical interpretations of the Confucian ethic, Hall and Ames (1987) have made important contributions in undermining collectivist interpretations of the ethic. I concur with them in holding that the best interpretations of Confucian ethics place relationships of mutual care and respect at the core of human fulfillment. To realize oneself is to be a self in relationship. It is not to lose the self in relationship or the larger group. Within the Confucian tradition, it is recognized that the interests of individuals, even in the best of relationships, can conflict. The ideal is to balance and reconcile the conflicting interests, and to do so in the light of the interdependence of individuals and of the goods they strive to realize. Sometimes one person's interests will have to yield to those of others. A partial compensation to that person is that a central part of their good lies in being, for instance, a member of the family. On the other hand, the good of the family cannot be achieved without consideration of an individual's important interests. If those interests are urgent and weighty, they must become important interests of the family and can sometimes have priority in case of conflict. At other times, differences have to be split in compromise. Sometimes yielding to others must be balanced against having priority at other times. In sum, one mutually adjusts conflicts in light of the interdependence of one's own good with that of others.

A story from 5A2 of the *Mencius* (*Mengzi* 2006–2021) illustrates these points. It is about Shun, a legendary sage-king exemplary for his ability to get people to work together and for his filial piety. When Shun wanted to get married, he knew that if he were to ask for his parents' permission to marry, he would be denied. He decided to marry anyway without telling them. Mencius defends what Shun did, saying that if Shun had let his parents deny him the most important of human relationships, it would have embittered him toward his parents. Shun's good as an individual depends on both his desired marriage relationship and his relationship to his parents. For him to conform to his parents' wishes is not only to deny him the first relationship but also to adversely affect the second. For the sake of both relationships he must assert his own good, which in the end is not separate from the good of his parents. Of course, one might well imagine that if one of his primary moral concerns was the health of his relationship with his parents, Shun would have had to have gone to considerable lengths to repair that relationship given what he had done, and he would be required to do this even if his parents had been unreasonably disposed against his marrying. The moral task in an ethic of relationships is often the task of finding a way to fulfill oneself in ways that also fulfill the community. In fact, it is the kind of project that Nelson Mandela very well described in talking about the ethics of Ubuntu: "[It] does not mean that people should not enrich themselves. The question therefore is, are you going to do so in order to enable the community around you, and enable it to improve?" (Mandela 2006).

A morality placing supreme value on the rights of individuals might well approach the problem of conflicts of interest in relationships differently, saying that Shun had every right to marry whomever he wanted to marry, and that he was under no obligation to repair his relationship with his parents. Thus, while it might endorse Shun's action of marrying anyway, it would have been for different reasons, and different subsequent actions might have been required. Note, however, that a relationship-oriented morality such as Confucianism does not differ from one that emphasizes the rights of the individual because it fails to recognize that important interests of the individual can conflict. It differs in its approach to dealing with such conflicts and in the weight it accords to the relationship as a constituent of each party's well-being. This does not mean that the interests of each individual are reduced to the interest in the relationship or that it can be acceptable to continually deny for the sake of the relationship the satisfaction of interests concerning matters other than that relationship.

As to the criticism that relationship-oriented moralities embody unacceptable hierarchies within the family, a number of contemporary defenders of the Confucian tradition have argued that the core ethical values of the tradition do not require objectionable kinds of subordination between men and women, husband and wife, or between parents and children. The earliest thinkers in the tradition, as represented by the *Mencius* and the *Analects* featuring the teachings of Confucius, did clearly accept the subordination of women to men, but did not attempt to justify it, and did not attribute to women capacities to realize virtue that are lesser than those possessed by men (see Chan 2000). Attempts came later to ground gender hierarchies in terms of a cosmology of the two main forces shaping the processes of change: *yin* (associated with the female) and *yang* (associated with the male). Though this cosmology has always portrayed the two forces as complementary and interdependent, the *yang* was also later conceived as superior and dominant over the *yin*. The Daoist tradition within Chinese thought, as it often does, serves as a corrective to the hierarchical tendencies of Confucian thought, and interrogates the conventional association of leadership with dominant attitudes and conduct. The *Daodejing* celebrates the efficacy of those who are receptive, responsive, self-effacing, and nurturing. Confucians can take on board much of that correction as wisdom about the true nature of leadership and who can become a leader.

Stereotypes of a moral tradition distant from one's own culture can often arise from "snapshots" taken from one perspective at a single stage of the tradition, which in turn are taken to represent the whole of that tradition. Many contemporary Confucians acknowledge the oppression embodied in the traditional gender roles that were endorsed by earlier Confucians and envision the core values of the tradition in ways that involve nonhierarchical reconceptualization of, for example, family roles. Marriage, for example, might be reconceived as based on friendship between partners, with each contributing according to their particular strengths and not because they are of a particular sex (see Rosenlee 2014 on what a contemporary dialogue between feminism, the care ethic, and Confucianism might look like).

The tendency to reify another moral tradition in terms of its earlier stages conflicts with the tendency to interpret one's own tradition in the light of meanings one judges it ought to have. Within the rights-centered tradition as embodied in the United States, for example, it is well known that the "self-evident truths" of the Declaration of Independence (US, 1776) do and do not greatly conflict with the practice and probably the intended meaning of the authors: "that all men are created equal, that they are endowed by their creator with unalienable Rights, that among these are Life, Liberty and the pursuit of Happiness." These words do not conflict in the sense that they really meant "men," not "women." They do conflict because "all men are created equal" did not mean the enslaved (including those enslaved by many of those who signed the Declaration), and they did not mean Native or First Americans. Further, the poor, even when of European origin, were widely thought to be a permanent underclass (see Richardson 2020). In fact, the authors probably meant to assert not the inalienable rights of individual human beings but the collective rights of the colonists to statehood and self-government (Rakove 2009).

Yet the words of the Declaration are now attributed the universal meanings pertaining to individuals that most contemporary Americans think they ought to have. And when the exclusions under "men" intended by the signers are acknowledged, the incongruence is elided through talk of inconsistency in thought and practice. The fact is that there has been real change, but continuing division of belief about the meaning of these "self-evident truths" that continues to this day, when considerable numbers of Americans do not honor the universalist interpretation in word or deed. If humility seems called for when pronouncing on what one's own moral tradition means, then it should be all the more called for when pronouncing what another's moral tradition means. If the meaning of one's own tradition is still in contention, one should also consider that others see their tradition as undergoing continuing contestation. Esme Murdock writes of the temporal perspective of settlers who have displaced Indigenous peoples that it "configures indigenous governance and sovereignty as firmly fixed in the chronological past and stagnating over time such that these governance structures and the political and legal philosophies that support them have stalled and not evolved or grown with the changing conditions of settler colonization and oppression" (Murdock 2022, 422).

As to the association of Confucianism with requiring unquestioning obedience of children to parents, such an interpretation is based more on common cultural practices than on the Confucian texts. It is true that the *Analects*, traditionally taken to be the most reliable reflection of the historical Confucius' teachings, sometimes (e.g., 1.11, 2.5 in *Analects* 2006–21) suggests unconditional obedience (though the passages are ambiguous, and there is plenty of controversy around the traditional assumption about the text's faithfulness to his teachings given the aggregative nature of the text, the product of many minds and hands). On the other hand, there is copious indication (4.18, 11.4, 13.15, 13.23, 14.22) that children have the responsibility to remonstrate with their parents if they believe them to be in error. The *Xiao Jing* or Classic of Filial Piety (*Xiao Jing* 2006–21, "Filial Piety in Relation to Reproof and Remonstrance"), characterizes remonstrating with a parent to dissuade them from unrighteous acts as required by loyalty to the parent, and the same holds, it is said, for the duties of a minister to a ruler, and a friend to a friend. Indeed, Xunzi, who articulated the most theoretically systematic version of Confucian ethics, and who was active near the end of the classical era, held that it was the moral responsibility of a child to *not* follow parental orders when following them, in contrast with disobeying them, would (1) endanger parents; (2) disgrace them; or (3) would be doing something beastly. The greatest filial piety, he declared, was understanding the proper purpose of following and not following orders (Xunzi 2006–21, "The Way of the Son").

7 Complicating the Contrast between Relationship- and Autonomy-Centered Moralities

Earlier, I characterized relationship- and autonomy-centered moralities as different from one another by comparing the degree of priority they put on the value of relationships as valued for their own sake with the degree of priority they put on the value of autonomy, especially personal autonomy to choose how to live, for its own sake. In characterizing my mother's implicit comparison of the Chinese attitude toward the worthwhile and meaningful life as one of fulfilling responsibilities to others versus broad latitude to do what one wanted in order to feel happiness (where happiness in her mind seemed to be a form of subjective contentment), I was contrasting an emphasis on relationship with an emphasis on personal autonomy. Growth of the network of responsibilities can be inversely related to broad latitude to do what one wants. It could be said that the responsibility dimension of relational valuing stands in an inverse relation to the *personal-choice* dimension of autonomy.

Recognizing this inverse relation between the two dimensions is compatible with recognizing other kinds of relation between them, depending on context. When discussing how increasing the scope and extent of one's responsibilities to others can have the effect of decreasing the scope of personal choice, we are assuming it is the same person whose responsibilities and personal choices are in question. However, there is also a sense in which the scope of personal choice can be expanded when others recognize and perform their responsibilities to the agent having personal choice. Most crucial are the responsibilities that need to be performed to enable a person to develop the capacities of agency. Human beings are born helpless, and only with the help of others do they become enabled to make choices and to act to fulfill them. Moreover, certain choices, such as the choice to pursue an advanced degree in physics, come into existence only when made possible and meaningful against the backdrop of practices and

institutions. And such practices and institutions are possible only with the appropriate responsibilities established and fulfilled to a sufficient degree. Thus certain kinds of responsibilities and their performance by the appropriate people may support personal autonomy for various others.

Furthermore, there are other dimensions of responsibility and autonomy that also give rise to different kinds of relationship to each other. Consider that besides personal autonomy, there is the moral autonomy of acting on one's moral judgment even if doing so displeases and contradicts the views of those in authority over oneself. Xunzi's view of what a son or minister should do when the father or ruler has done or is about to do something quite wrong is an example of such moral autonomy. Here again, being in certain kinds of relationship, such as having a model and teacher who encourages disagreement and argument with him in the way Confucius did in the *Analects* (see 2.9, 9.30, 13.23, 15.36), can help nurture such moral autonomy. There are few formulations of the ethical life in any tradition, I would maintain, that rival Confucius' answer to his students' question about his aspirations in life: "To comfort the aged, to engender trust in my friends, and to nurture the young" (*Analects* 5.26).

The comparison of rich and complex moral traditions is itself a rich and complex task. Interpreting a moral tradition deeply is to identify its central values, and, unavoidably, it is to judge which articulations of that tradition have been the most plausible in terms of those central values. Inquiry into whether there is a single true morality involves such interpretation and comparison, and in this regard, the argument departs from the way most metaethicists ply their trade. They mostly aspire to stay above the fray and avoid answering the question, "Well, does this particular tradition make plausible claims about what a good human life is, and about what it is to act rightly? If so, can we say that these claims are more plausible than ones to be found in other moral traditions?" The attempt to stay above the fray of engaging in these questions has led to unproductive discussions that do not engage with the importance of morality in human life.

If the job of interpreting and comparing moral traditions is done correctly, I maintain, one will find familiar ideas, often in unfamiliar contexts, and differences intertwined with similarities. Confucian ethics generally does not highly value personal autonomy, and that is because its vision of a flourishing human life is that of relationship and responsibility to others. Its de-emphasis on personal autonomy places it in contrast with familiar versions of what I call autonomy- and rights-centered traditions, but I have pointed out the strong presence of another kind of autonomy that should be familiar to thoughtful advocates of rights-centered traditions, which I have called moral autonomy. Confucian ethics, or important strands of its tradition, do recognize that the interests of individuals, though such interests include as central elements relationship to others and contribution to the good of community, do come into conflict with those relationships, with the interests of others with whom one is in relationship, and with the good of community. This conflict may or may not be fully resolved. But the resources it brings to these problems are formidable.

Once one begins to probe into the issues and arguments of a tradition, it is possible to see lines of thought that are not only intelligible but cogent. One may not arrive at the same set of priorities the other tradition may be tending toward, but one may be impressed, as I was when I began to study the Chinese tradition, by the range of familiar and important considerations to which that tradition responds, and by the dimensions of value to which it can attach importance, and do so for good reasons. It is partly because other traditions can overlap with one's own concerns, and bring forward lines of reasoning and apt response to them, that one can begin to form appreciation for alternative forms of thought and practice that both converge and diverge from the tradition(s) with which one is more familiar. One begins to see alternative pathways and feels less assurance that there is or needs to be a single correct pathway for human beings.

More specifically, once one investigates how a tradition that tilts in favor of relationship deals with major challenges, and to the extent one can do the same for a tradition that tilts in favor of (personal) autonomy, one not only sees that the issue between them is more subtle than initially construed, but also that one might also see how ways of life realizing each type of tradition might offer fulfilling human lives. In Section 21, I will address the issue of what a better version of the rights-centered tradition in its American version might look like when it deals with problems in its conception of rights. To the extent that one conducts such a comparison, and finds plausible and formidable versions of each tradition, one might begin to doubt that one tradition should be declared the winner.

One might also doubt, to address another possibility, that there is some single ideal balancing point that combines the strengths of the traditions and avoids the moral downsides that each is prone to have. The responsibilities toward families in Mencius' discussion of Shun's marriage prod individuals to engage in the give-and-take of staying in relationship while working on the inevitable problems encountered. As seen from Mencius' reasoning about the course of action Shun took, staying in relationship need not involve suppressing one's own urgent desires and needs, and if one successfully reconciles these desires and needs with maintaining viable relationships with important others, then greater fulfillment may be achieved. But the challenges can be steep, and the chances of failure not insignificant. Looking at this second possibility, lowering moral expectations of what is required in relationship, or of what is required to sustain it, looks appealing, and recognizing a strong right to exit a relationship without having to work through reconciling its demands with one's pressing desires and needs is a way to do that. Yet reducing or lowering expectations of what is required in relationship can encourage people to part ways too soon rather than putting the work into making the relationship work.

The best hope for there being a single true or most justified morality is the idea of an optimal configuration of values that somehow combines the normative appeal of all of them. To the extent to which there is need to prioritize values when they come into conflict, the optimal morality would set the correct priorities. To some extent, this possible route to universalism is the most appealing to me, and this might not be surprising, given my bicultural background. It also appeals to my sense of what is going wrong with the American experiment in democracy and individual rights. During various points in US history, the country has made significant progress in extending the promise of equality of rights and of acknowledging the equal dignity of all, but equally often, it has shown that its upholding of rights tends to favor some and not others, and that its rhetorical affirmation of equal dignity is underlain by relegation of some to an underclass from which it is extremely difficult to escape because of race, economic background, and gender. It has most recently seemed to generate many divisive battles over what rights people have and what they are entitled to do under those rights. These problems can be addressed, I argue in Sections 21–22, and part of the path to successfully doing so is through taking the value of relationship more seriously, and in particular the need to accommodate others even when there is serious disagreement in order to continue making a life with them. It is part of my view that different moral traditions can learn from each other and yet still retain their distinctive identities.

Arriving at such conclusions might produce an experience that could be called "moral ambivalence" (Wong 2006), by which one becomes significantly uncertain as to whether there is a singular truth as to how to balance or prioritize values that are shared across different moral traditions. To clarify the way that ambivalence is deployed in the argument: There is no claim that everyone or even most people have had this experience. The experience deserves epistemic weight in proportion to the understanding achieved by the subject of the experience. Ambivalence can be gotten on the cheap or it can be earned. Further, there can be no assurance that those of comparable understanding will have similar reactions of ambivalence when addressing the same conflict. When experienced by those who have seriously and in a sustained fashion sought understanding of what is to be said for all reasonable sides, ambivalence puts pressure on inquirers for an explanation.

The experience of moral ambivalence does not, by any means, prove the truth of relativism, but presents an explanatory challenge that relativist or universalist theories might satisfy in varying degrees and different ways.[2] If there is a single right way to deal with difficult conflicts of value, relativists ask universalists what they think that single right way is and why they think it is so. If their answers rest on the intuition of some set of "self-evident" truths, the relativist may further ask why that intuition should be favored over others that have lain at the core of other traditions, or even the intuitions of others in their own tradition.

Some universalists and realists assert that disagreeing parties might never be able to resolve their differences even in epistemically ideal circumstances (McGrath 2010). If one is a robust realist, it is argued, then one must be prepared to admit an epistemic gap that is unbridgeable, at least in our current circumstances. Such a possibility cannot be refuted, but perhaps it gives up too soon on the project of explanation, for it is unclear on such a view where the line falls between the humanly knowable and unknowable, the uresolvable and unresolvable: Does it fall between those disagreements that seem to hinge only on disagreement over nonmoral factual questions (the knowable) and those disagreements that seem to involve differences over moral values (the unknowable)? If so, that leaves a huge domain of unknowability. If the domain of unknowability is smaller (somewhere within the class of disagreements involving differences over moral values), how is the boundary drawn?

Relativists often press the case against universalism by advancing a view of morality that can be called naturalistic. Here, naturalism about morality is deployed as part of the theoretical framework used to present what is claimed to be the best explanation of the moral ambivalence just described. In the next Sections, this naturalism is explained and combined with the phenomenon of moral ambivalence to argue for a moderate form of moral relativism or strong form of moral pluralism.

8 The Underdiscussed Question of What Morality Is

Someone outside academic moral philosophy might justifiably assume that the question of what morality is would be one of the most thoroughly discussed topics in that discipline. This turns out not to be the case. Much argumentation and theorizing about morality is premised on a conception of morality that is treated as a definition or that is virtually equivalent to one. Michael Smith argues from the "platitudes"– that morality is about objective facts and that

---

[2] These clarifications of how I think moral ambivalence should come about so as to have weight in the argument for relativism were inspired by critical points made by Christopher Gowans (2007) in a review of Wong (2006).

when people make moral judgments they are motivated to act on them – to the conclusion that moral judgments are judgments about what one would desire if one were rational (Smith 1994). On the other hand, J. L. Mackie (1977) starts from a conception of morality as concerning objective moral facts and in which these facts are objectively prescriptive (they unconditionally give any one reasons to behave morally) to the conclusion that there can be no true moral judgments because there are no such facts and no such objective prescriptivity. He asserts that these features are part of the ordinary conception of morality and embedded in the meanings of moral terms, as well as being acknowledged by many moral philosophers. The problem with such arguments is that the conceptions of morality they presuppose are mainly based on the philosopher's intuitions about the judgments and inferences that laypeople make (see Gil 2009; Sarkissian 2017).

Empirical work on laypeople's concepts of morality throws such philosophical arguments under the suspicion of being parochial. Geoffrey Goodwin and John Darley (2008) devised measures to gauge people's beliefs in moral objectivity. The extent to which one tends to treat a moral judgment as true or false and to believe there is one correct answer as to whether that judgment is true or false is an indication of the degree of objectivity one assigns to the judgment. When queried on the truth of various judgments on an array of ethical issues, participants varied considerably in assigning truth value *according to the kind of act being judged*. Most strikingly, although they generally agreed with the permissibility of abortion, assisted death, and stem-cell research, only very small percentages assigned truth values to the judgments expressing their views (2008, 1346). In a second experiment, Goodwin and Darley asked participants whether there was one correct answer as to whether a moral judgment was true or not. The participants were far more willing to say there was a correct answer as to the wrongness of robbing a bank than they were to say the same about the goodness of anonymous giving and were highly unlikely to claim a correct answer as to the permissibility of assisted death (2008, 1352). The participants' reluctance to attribute truth to the latter moral judgment may stem from two thoughts they might have had: recognition that opposing answers on matters such as the permissibility of abortion, assisted death, and stem-cell research might be equally reasonable; and the assumption that conflicting positions cannot both be true. When given the opportunity to say that there is more than one correct answer as to whether a moral judgment about these issues is true or not, significant numbers of participants took that opportunity.

The Goodwin and Darley study suggests that there is a diversity of attitudes toward the objectivity of moral judgments, not just across people, but also across the range of ethical issues and possible subjects of disagreement.

Wright et al. (2013) asked participants to classify topics as factual, moral, conventional, or a matter of taste. They found no difference between average levels of imputed objectivism for the items participants classified as moral. Wright and her colleagues confirmed the diversity of attitudes on moral objectivity, which they call "meta-ethical pluralism." Strikingly, Goodwin and Darley found that the strongest beliefs in the objective correctness of morality tend to be held by those who believe them to be the commands of God, not the source of objectivity to be expected from reading Smith or Mackie. The results of these studies have adverse implications for a customary way that universalists often argue for their metaethical position: that it is inherent to the very concept of morality that it is about objective facts that admit of a single true answer. In fact, characteristics attributed to morality are not only as disputable to laypeople as they are to philosophers, but laypeople are also liable to respond in diverse ways to the fact of moral disagreements and to perceived difficulties in resolving certain kinds of such disagreements.

One of the ways that philosophers typically do metaethics is as an exercise in conceptual analysis. As the arguments of Smith and Mackie demonstrate, this conceptual analysis of moral concepts rests on the assumption that the concepts are uniform and stable across the populations of their users, which may be why philosophers feel free to rely on their own intuitions about conceptual contents. This assumption looks simply to be wrong. It gives less credit to laypeople than they deserve. Thoughtful people can be expected to continue thinking about what sort of thing morality is, and their observations about moral disagreements and how and whether they have been resolved may indeed affect their views about some of the most basic characteristics they attribute to morality. In addition, people's larger views about the nature of the world and its origins may affect their views about the nature of morality. Those who adhere to a strongly theistic view may adhere to a divine-command theory of morality, regardless of most philosophers since Plato's *Euthyphro* having accepted that the gods approve of something because it is right, rather than something's being right because the gods approve of it.

9 A Naturalistic Approach to Understanding Why Human Beings Have Moralities

Rather than simply relying on conceptual analysis, this Element proposes to ask why morality seems so important and central to human life, drawing from the most relevant human sciences in looking for answers. This is what is meant by taking a naturalistic approach. Sometimes a naturalistic approach is associated with the attempt to reduce all phenomena to the physical. The approach adopted here does not attempt to do that. Instead, it seeks only to make best use of the relevant sciences to explain the phenomena in question. This "methodological" naturalism, as opposed to a reductive or "substantive" naturalism (see Railton 1989; Wong 2006), furthermore, does not seek to reduce all normative concepts to descriptive ones. For one thing, the standards or norms that govern scientific inquiry may not be reducible to nonnormative properties. Normative concepts may receive definition only in terms of other normative concepts. Scanlon (1998), for example, argues that the concept of a reason (to believe or to do something) may only be explicated in terms of phrases such as "a consideration counting in favor of."

The aim here is not to reduce but to clarify what kinds of reasons morality provides as it guides thought and action. The proposal here is that a very large class of moral reasons direct us to cooperate with each other. Here, I draw from the scientific understanding of how the human biological inheritance prepares us for cooperation. We share with the great apes a capacity for empathy with others and for reciprocating the good they do for us (Flack and de Waal 2000; de Waal 2008), suggesting a shared evolutionary history resulting in genetically based dispositions for these behaviors. However, humans are distinctively equipped with dispositions to develop complex cognitive and emotional traits that enable them to cooperate at levels of far greater scale, coordination, and complexity (Tomasello 2019).

Within human evolutionary theory, there has been a great deal of activity in generating hypotheses as to how human beings could have evolved other-concerned and reciprocating motivations. There are hypotheses as to why human beings might be disposed to act for the sake of their kin at cost to themselves (Hamilton 1964), why they tend to reciprocate cooperation with cooperation (Trivers 1971), why they might be disposed to engage in personally costly acts of punishing others who free ride on the cooperation of others (Gintis 2000), and why they might engage in personally costly acts for the sake of nonrelated others (Sober and Wilson 1998; for an update on later work that builds on these hypotheses, see Okasha 2020). Besides forms of reciprocity that are highly conditional and transactional in nature, reciprocity can take place in kin and other kinds of relationships encompassing bonds of care and affection, and these bonds can also have an evolutionary basis (see Hrdy 2011). These hypotheses help explain how human beings became adapted for a life of cooperation with each other, in part through evolved capacities to have concern for others and to be disposed to help them (Hrdy 2011; Tomasello 2019).

Physically, we are unprepossessing animals, easily preyed upon by larger, quicker, stronger animals with sharp teeth. Cooperating with each other, however, we multiply our powers manifold. While our closest relations, the great apes, show some social motivations, such as empathy, they largely treat each other instrumentally as means to their individual ends, especially outside their families. Human beings not only have the capacities to care about others for their own sake, but also have genetically based dispositions to create and to follow cultural norms with prosocial content, and these norms support and greatly enhance motivations to cooperate (Richerson et al. 2003; Richerson and Boyd 2005; Tomasello 2019). Such motivations, together with self-interest and the tendency to favor members of one's own group(s), constitute a diverse array of propensities that make cooperation possible but often pose problems of motivational conflict for human beings. Morality could be that part of human culture, a set of norms, practices, and judgments of various degrees of generality that is used to socialize and guide human beings toward productive forms of cooperation (Curry et al. 2019).[3]

Moralities can have other functions that overlap with the function of fostering cooperation. These other functions prescribe ideals of character and striving after values that are sometimes independent of or go beyond what is needed for social cooperation (in my comment on Curry et al. 2019, appended to that essay, I make this point). They spell out what a good or fulfilling or flourishing way of life is, and what kind of character is needed to live that way. Such ideals serve the need for a kind of intrapersonal coordination among the individual's diverse motivations such as concern for others, concern for self, and the self's projects and commitments. Anyone with young children is familiar with their alternation of clashing motivations in quick and seemingly arbitrary succession. Internal motivational conflict is a common phenomenon of human life, and so is the feeling of frustration at having defeated oneself by pursuing first one end and then another, incompatible end, through indecision and wavering between one's desires. Human culture attempts to bring motivational conflict under control through ideals of the good and worthwhile life that identify the ends most worthy of pursuit. For example, knowledge, affectionate relationships, and fulfillment of responsibilities to others are quite often marked as constituents of a good human life, and guiding oneself by these values can foster reasonable coherence (I say "reasonable coherence" because it is not an exact or purely logical matter to make a consistent whole of diverse ends that may come into

---

[3] Sharon Street (2006) invokes the influence of evolutionary forces on the content of evaluative judgments in arguing against robust realism, which is the view that there are evaluative truths existing independent of any evaluative attitudes. The form of pluralism defended here also denies such a robust realism, but the argument for it depends on a conception of the functions of morality that is not much in evidence in Street's work (perhaps because she is focused on the status of "evaluative judgments" in general). In my argument, I connect the function of facilitating and regulating cooperation with hypotheses about the adaptiveness of evolved dispositions that prime human beings to cooperate.

conflict with one another in the unpredictable circumstances of an ongoing life). Moralities also sometimes contain ideals of how people should relate to those parts of their environment that are not human, animal, plant, or even water, as seen above in the references to some of the ethics of African and Indigenous peoples, and to Daoism in the Chinese tradition, though again, these ideals may contribute to the viability of cooperation between humans, for example in fostering an appreciation for the nonhuman environment that makes for sustainability in resources and that supports cooperation. However, human beings have attained deep and lasting satisfaction in being able to live in relationships to nonhuman environments that they can regard as their homes.

10 Putting Together Moral Ambivalence and a Naturalistic Conception of Morality

This section puts together the two parts of the argument for a kind of metaethical moral relativism: moral ambivalence and a naturalistic conception of morality as constructed. Recall from Section 7 that the relevant kind of moral ambivalence is the result of serious and sustained inquiry into moralities that give conflicting answers to some of the most pressing moral problems. Another component of the argument is the conception of morality as emerging from human biology and culture to foster and regulate social cooperation and internal motivational coherence between the differing and potentially conflicting kinds of motivation within individuals. The argument in this section is that this naturalistic constructivist conception of morality, when combined with constraints on what can be an adequate morality that fulfills its functions, will provide the most plausible explanation of moral ambivalence.

Ambivalence is coming to see other moralities as alternatives to one's own. If these others are alternatives to one's own, then these others and one's own must have something fundamentally in common. On the conception of morality advanced here, they all are ways of promoting and sustaining interpersonal cooperation and internal motivational coherence. If in fact there is not just one correct way for moralities to perform these functions, moral ambivalence would be the result. The claim here is that some version of metaethical relativism – that there is no single true morality – emerges as part of the best explanation of moral ambivalence. This kind of argument from the best explanation does not purport to be definitive in the way that the conclusion deductively follows from self-evident premises. Because it makes a claim for a certain theory about morality as part of the best explanation, it is subject to comparison with other candidates for the best explanation, including universalist ones claiming there is a single true morality. In the next section, I add other components to this theory of morality that I think strengthen the claim that it is the best explanation, and these are components that yield constraints on what could be a true morality. There is a plurality of true moralities, but it is a bounded plurality.

11 Constraints on the Range of Viable Moralities

As noted in Section 1, a debate is shaped by the way that its participants frame the question to be debated, which in turn shapes the conceptions of the alternatives in play. The debate over metaethical relativism has tended to oscillate between extremes. On one extreme is an "anything goes" sort of relativism. It might be a moral subjectivism that hinges moral truth or justifiability solely on the individual's adopted standards. It might be a social conventionalism that directs us to the group's standards. On the other extreme sits a robust universalism, according to which moral properties are conceived on the model of physical properties that exist independently of all human thought and decision. Alternatively, morality consists of laws of pure practical reason applying to any rational being, human or nonhuman. Sometimes those on the universalist side of the spectrum make a move toward the middle without explicitly acknowledging that they are doing so. For example, some grant that certain moral problems may lack a truth-apt resolution due to vagueness in moral concepts (Shafer-Landau 1994, 1995, 2003), or because of ties in the ranking of moral values that come into conflict (Brink 1989), or because of the noncomparability of such values (Shafer-Landau 1994, 1995, 2003). But they tend to put these admissions into parentheses. For relativists, including this author, who make a move toward the middle and acknowledge doing so (Wong 2006; Velleman 2013), the conception of morality as functioning to promote human cooperation is the key. The function of fostering cooperation, when combined with widespread and typical human propensities that may have been selected as adaptive, may produce objective constraints on morality (Wong 2006).

The function of coordinating intrapersonal motivations may, in combination with the character of widespread and typical human propensities, also be a source of objective constraint, but the range of what human beings have regarded as a good and worthwhile life is wide and encompasses such diverse ends that it is difficult to identify the function of intrapersonal coordination of motivation as a purely independent source of constraint on true moralities, apart from the way that prioritizing such ends as the fulfillment of responsibilities to others as a central constituent of the good life can also help fulfill the interpersonal function of facilitating cooperation. For example, those ideals of the good life that place limits on the legitimacy of pursuing one's self-interest, especially of doing so at the cost of others' interests, will clearly also advance the interpersonal function of facilitating and regulating cooperation. Hence the focus will be on the argument from the interpersonal function.

Let us return to the idea that morality is a normative guide that arose partly to foster social cooperation. Consider that not any form of social cooperation could plausibly be deemed moral. Forms of cooperation such as slavery that are sustainable only through threats of harm or through deception are not morally acceptable because of the type of normative guide morality is supposed to be, which is a guide that can be accepted on a voluntary basis by appeal to interests (not necessarily or not only self-interests) that human beings typically or characteristically have. This is plausibly one of the meanings of "morality" (Wong 2019b).

Given the earlier criticism of claims about morality made on the basis of pure conceptual analysis, it is appropriate to be modest about the claim that morality is a normative guide that should not depend on deception or coercion for acceptance. While it is likely quite a common belief about morality, not all such beliefs can be put together into a coherent and explanatorily useful theory of morality. Consider Goodwin and Darley's finding, mentioned in Section 8, that quite a few people think of morality as composed of God's commands, and the apparent link between this thought and a very strong form of objectivity that these people attribute to morality. A divine-command theory of morality would rule out many of the explanatorily useful points about morality, biological and cultural evolution, and cooperation that have been made in this Element. A coherent theory will probably have to be somewhat revisionist in its intent (Gibbard 1992), and will not give full credit to the beliefs that some number of people have about morality.

The aim is to account for the broadest set of the beliefs about morality that appear to be the most plausible, given what else is known about the human world and beyond. The constraint that morality be acceptable on a voluntary basis, not dependent on coercion or deception, enables a theory that incorporates the way a great deal of moral criticism has been made and that has enabled genuine change in human history, for example, criticism of theories of race and gender that attribute inferior capacities of rationality or self-control to whole groups of human beings, theories which were then utilized to subordinate those groups.

To be clear, the proposed constraint on what a true morality could be is not based on a contractualist view of the origin of morality. There is no claim that morality emerges from agreements that people make with each other to cooperate in certain ways. Rather, the claim is that morality is a normative guide that purports to be acceptable to those who come under its governance on grounds free of coercion or deception. We might then say that a morality that can be accepted only under conditions of coercion or deception cannot be a true morality. We might then call this universal constraint on all moralities "justifiability to the governed." This constraint leaves open the matter of what grounds people could have to accept a morality without coercion or deception, but some of the earlier discussion of the content of relationship- or autonomy-centered moralities suggests possible grounds: Relationships of the right sort plausibly form much of the substance of a meaningful human life; the personal autonomy to have control over how one lives one's life also has deep and wide appeal.

Other constraints on what could be a true or justifiable morality do not derive from the meaning of the concept of morality but from its function of sustaining voluntary social cooperation together with the widespread and typical psychological propensities of human beings (what could be called "human nature," but without the essentialist implication that every member of the species must possess all such psychological propensities). If one of these widespread and typical propensities, self-interest, promises to render social cooperation problematic, then true or justifiable moralities will have to address this challenge, and this will be done partly through the content of their norms. A norm of reciprocity, in particular a norm requiring people to return good for good received, might be a necessary component of all true moralities that helps to relieve the psychological burden of contributing to social cooperation when it comes into conflict with self-interest. It takes some pressure off other-regarding concern as a motivation for cooperation.

A reciprocity norm can take many specific forms that can vary with the particular morality and with the type of relationship they apply to. It can apply to a more purely transactional relationship that is based on particular benefits given and that can require tit-for-tat, in-kind return. It can also apply to relationships based on kinship or friendship, in which purely transactional exchange might be regarded as contrary to or destructive of the relationship. Rather, appropriate return for benefit received might be conceived as adjusted to what the recipient, in their particular circumstances, is capable of giving back. A child is not expected, for example, to return in-kind benefits to a parent who cares for and nurtures them. In some cultures, the return might take the form of receptivity to the parent's direction, affection, and acknowledgment of what was given by the parent (see Earp et al. 2021 for an empirically informed discussion of "transactional" versus "care-based" forms of reciprocity).

A third constraint concerns "accommodation," a value that might have to be acknowledged within all adequate moralities fulfilling the function of fostering interpersonal cooperation, because of the ubiquity of disagreement over how to interpret even those values that might be shared among people or how to prioritize values in case of conflict. This value is a willingness to maintain a constructive relationship with others with whom one is in serious and even intractable disagreement. Social cooperation would come under impossible pressure if it always depended on strict agreement (see chapters 2 and 9 in Wong 2006 for further discussion). As a moral value, accommodation expresses a primal form of respect for others that transcends any requirement that they agree with one. Antonio Cua (1989) identifies the presence of this value in Confucian ethics, and it is given prominent expression by the *Analects* passage in which Confucius says of the exemplary person, the primary moral ideal in that text, that such a person pursues harmony rather than sameness; the petty person does the opposite (13.23). In this respect, all adequate moralities must have this value of relationship.

The three constraints identified are substantial but do not narrow the possibilities to one single true morality. Justifiability to the governed leaves a range of moralities that might be accepted without coercion or deception. Reciprocating good for good and accommodation, while not subject to arbitrary or whimsical interpretation, can be interpreted in significantly different ways in different moralities, and their relative priorities compared to other values would also be subject to variation. How a morality addresses these issues determines its more specific content, and the range of moralities that satisfy the general constraints in different ways and in different forms constitute the plurality of true or most justified moralities.

Aside from universal constraints arising from the combination of the cooperative function and human propensities, the truth conditions of moral judgments are shaped by local and contingent factors. A deeper explanation will refer to the complexity and variety of human needs and desires and how they can evolve to take different forms in particular circumstances. Further, because of the variety of human motivations, the ability to strike different balances between, for example, needs for relationship and for personal autonomy makes for a range of different ways to live deeply satisfying human lives. The case for pluralism and against universalism may ultimately be supported by reflection on the tension between values such as relationship and autonomy, individual rights and the greater good, and the duties of special relationship and duties to human beings (or perhaps all sentient beings) as such. The tension between such values can certainly be ameliorated, and in some circumstances, these values can be compatible and even mutually reinforcing, but as Isaiah Berlin observed, we can envision no utopia in which the maximal realizations of these values are made compatible with one another (Berlin 2002, 212–217).

The universalist might insist that there must be a single correct balance between all the important values, but then the problem, as discussed earlier in relation to moral ambivalence, is to specify in what the balance consists and how to justify that there is such a singular ideal balance. The task of balancing is liable to be much more complex and the options more numerous when we recognize that it is not trying to bring into alignment simply and broadly specified values such as relationship, autonomy, and rights. There are different kinds of relationships (e.g., those of the family, friendship, those defined by institutional roles such as professor and student), different kinds of rights that can have varying scopes (with variation in the scopes being a major way of balancing rights against each other or against other nonrights considerations such as public welfare). The sheer number and variety of ways to finely parse values strongly suggests that there is a significant plurality of viable options for combining and balancing them.

Development of this idea that morality is socially constructed, but constrained around the functions of promoting and sustaining social cooperation and fostering internal motivational coherence within the individual, must address some major questions, addressed in the following Sections: Who does the constructing? And within the range of plural moralities defined by the universal constraints of adequacy, when there is conflict in what they require and encourage people to be and to do, can we call that conflict *disagreement*?

12 The Social Construction of Morality: By the Individual or Group?

This section gives an answer more specifically to the question of who socially constructs morality. The individual? The group? The theory defended here is not that the morality of a group is a single set of norms to which all members of a group subscribe. The set of norms, practices, and judgments that come to be called a morality has imprecise and varying borders, and its various constituents will be subject to varying interpretations and disagreements. At times, depending on the context and aim of inquiry, one might talk about American or Chinese morality, but it must always be kept in mind that such descriptors comprehend considerable internal diversity. As seen from the discussion of Confucian ethics, which is itself part of a complex and diverse Chinese moral tradition, there is considerable variety of views expressed among Confucians on crucial issues such as the requirements of filial piety.

Some critics of relativism have called attention to the difficulty of drawing clear and unqualified boundaries for the morality of any given group or society (Moody-Adams 1997). Some relativists are vulnerable to that charge given the way they conceive of how true moralities can vary across groups. Gilbert Harman (1975), for example, influentially suggested that moralities consist of implicit agreement among members of a group to intend to act in certain ways on the conditions that others similarly intend. His theory seems to presuppose a uniformity of basic moral commitments among members of the relevant group.

David Velleman (2013) has argued for a form of moral relativism that construes moralities as specifying the action-types that are "doable" within a given community. To learn the morality of a community is to learn what sorts of action make sense or are intelligible for agents in that community. For Velleman, then, adherents to different moralities will not even be able to understand what passes as "doable" in each other's moralities. Rovane (2013), like Velleman, holds a version of relativism based on the mutual unintelligibility of various moral worlds. She gives an example in the contrast between the hypothetical Anjali, who lives a life of traditional duties to family and obedience to parents' wishes in a rural village of Punjab in India, and a hypothetical middle-class American woman who grows up in a small town in middle America, goes to a distinguished university, earns an advanced degree, and goes into a business career. She does not marry, contrary to her parents' wishes, and does not think she is morally obliged to comply with those wishes. Anjali, on the other hand, submits to the marriage her parents arranged for her. While Rovane grants that these two different moral worlds may share "moral platitudes" in common, such as the general wrongness of killing, harming, and hindering agency, she argues that such points of agreement are too general to be action-guiding.

It is true that culture gives specific substance as to when one should specifically refrain from killing, harming, and hindering, and what specifically counts as such actions. However, this does not mean that different moral "worlds" are hermetically sealed from one another (see Appiah 2006; Wong 2006). The businesswoman in Rovane's example grew up in a small town and was raised by parents who wished her to marry. She knows something of the specifics of the traditional world of her parents. Or in Velleman's terms, she knows what is "doable" in that world. Many Americans live in the interface between these two worlds. In India, many young people are now imbued with an ethic that prizes personal autonomy, yet many of them opt for marriages arranged by their families and professional matchmakers. Cultures of the urban and the rural sit cheek by jowl, and considerable numbers of people are conversant with both. Matchmakers help young people to navigate and cross bridges between them.

British-born Indians generate a variety of marriage-making practices, from one extreme at which the children do not even have a veto over their parents' choices of mates, to the other extreme in which parents are only involved in staging the wedding. The most popular choices within this group are in between: the semiarranged marriage in which parents select potential mates and introduce them to their children, after which a courtship ensues in which the children are encouraged to fall in love; and the "love-cum-arranged marriage" in which the children first select their potential mates on their own, then introduce them to their parents to get a parental-approved introduction and courtship. These choices in the middle of the spectrum reflect a desire to accept in some ways the traditional constraint of parental approval of spouses for children, together with the freedom to fall in love on one's own (Pande 2021).

To sum up, a challenge for the kind of group-based relativism that is based on the idea that different groups do not disagree but rather cannot understand each other in some fundamental way is that when examined more deeply, the kinds of examples given actually undermine the conclusion they are supposed to support. People within each group disagree with each other, and their moral ideas can substantially overlap with the ideas of people in other groups.

To take another example of what is usually regarded as a deep moral disagreement, those who are pro-life and pro-choice on abortion don't necessarily have the problem of understanding the other side's position, but the intractability of this sort of disagreement has been one of the main grounds to take relativism seriously. Sometimes the disagreement over abortion is explained in terms of disagreement over nonmoral facts pertaining to the morality of abortion, for example, whether there is a God who has endowed humanity with the divine purpose of procreation and who confers souls at conception or shortly thereafter. While some may ground their anti-abortion stance on such a belief, not everyone with this stance does so, and may instead point to obligations to protect developing, or at least potential, human life. As shall be seen in Sections 21–22, there is again a spectrum of positions on the morality of abortion that involves a mix of normative considerations – the necessity of respecting actual or potential life versus the autonomy of the pregnant person – that are comprehensible and often given moral force on both sides.

The challenges for conceiving morality as constructed by groups might lead one to adopt a more individualistic version of relativism. James Dreier (1990) and Jesse Prinz (2007) have defended a version of what Drier labels "speaker relativism," according to which the content of moral terms is determined by the individual speaker's moral commitments (or in Dreier's language "motivating attitudes"). Given such an analysis, however, it becomes problematic to explain why people treat a speaker's moral pronouncements as typically having implications for what *they* have moral reason to approve and to do. Such implications may be rejected, especially if the speaker's pronouncements seem way out of line with the audience's conception of appropriate judgment in the circumstances the speaker is addressing, but it often takes this kind of stark incongruence to upset the expected implications. Most of the actual cases of moral disagreement are not of this extreme variety, but blend the familiar with the different. The upshot is that morality often bears an interpersonal dimension that belies the conception of morality as speaker-relative (for more on this topic, see Wong 2011, 2019a).

These implications from the speaker to the audience are especially liable to be drawn in contexts where people are engaged in cooperation to accomplish a common project. Michael Tomasello (2019) writes of "joint commitments" in which people perceive in each other a commitment to act together and to also agree on the appropriateness of sanction from the participants on whomever does not fulfill the role ideal assigned to each participant. This is clearest in small-scale, face-to-face collaborations, and as the scale of human cooperation broadens to encompass cooperation with people one does not see and does not even know, culture provides moral norms to specify the responsibilities and prerogatives of one's role ideal. Even on the large and impersonal scale, it is not unusual for people to think that sanction is appropriate for someone unknown to them but who is simply described as not doing their part. Such reactions are consistent with the hypothesis that morality is intimately involved in the furtherance of cooperation, and since the scale and complexity of cooperation makes it arguably the activity that most distinctively and consistently distinguishes human beings from all other life on earth, it is plausible to see it as enmeshed with the nature of morality. But now there is a puzzle. If morality is not the sole expression of a speaker's prescriptions or of a group that is monolithically united around a set of norms and distinguished from other groups who occupy different moral worlds, then what is it?

There is an alternative to regarding morality as the possession of a group or of the individual. We need not treat them as dichotomous alternatives. This alternative involves recognizing that in human cooperative life, there is need to regulate and convey to all participants what is expected of them, but also considerable play in how these expectations are interpreted by individuals and subgroups. The norms, often implicit, that spell out expectations can be fluid, often vague, and in need of further specification and interpretation. Sometimes cooperation is on the large scale of encompassing a whole society or even societies or nations, and sometimes it is on a very small scale, within a family or neighborhood. People may draw from the conceptual resources utilized to regulate and foster cooperation on one of these levels and argue that these resources are applicable to another level of cooperation. Confucian ethics often gives rise to arguments in which moral resources regularly applied to the family level are said to be applicable to larger levels. Arguments from analogy can play a crucial role, starting with a context of cooperation in which, say, certain kinds of duties or responsibilities are widely accepted as having force, and then moving to another context in which this is not so obvious, but where the argument is meant to point to relevant similarities with the first context. This provides opportunity for the individual to exercise their own creative and interpretive thought. Such thought can go into justifications to others of the moral acceptability of what the individual has done or proposes to do, with implications for the acceptability of others' actions.

These characteristics of morality arise because of the complexity and variety of the people and groups it serves to guide. Morality plausibly arises from customs and practices that emerge and evolve implicitly (most of the time) among people who belong to more than one group. This is especially true of modern, large societies with populations diverse in ethnicity and social class. Even much smaller and simpler societies are subject to significant diversity of group membership that introduces diversity of moral belief. The Greek tragedy *Antigone* (Sophocles 1984) is about values of family loyalty and obedience to the gods (which requires that Antigone bury the body of her brother) and the value of political loyalty to the state (King Creon has declared the brother a traitor and that he not be buried). We, like Antigone, have choices to make between the conflicting demands of the groups to which we belong. Both the group and the individual are factors in the moralities we end up having. Neither "morality is determined by the group" nor "morality is determined by the individual" seem right as mutually exclusive options.

In this respect, moral language is like natural language in general. Just as natural languages have no clear and unqualified boundaries (they have dialects and even idiolects of individual speakers who inherit a shared language but develop some idiosyncratic meanings for parts of that shared language), the meanings of terms change over time and new terms get incorporated from other natural languages. Similarly, moral languages have a social origin that is diverse and dynamic. We learn what terms such as 'good person' and 'right action' mean from those who raise us, but also from those who school us, our peers, and other social influences. Though there might very well be some measure of agreement between these different sources, such agreement inevitably coexists with diversity, even of the fundamental kind that does not depend on difference in nonmoral factual belief, so that different people in our fields of social influence do not mean precisely the same things when they use moral terms. From common experience, we know that cooperation with others does not require uniformity of normative belief (in Section 22, there are striking examples of such cooperation).

13 When People Differ in Their Moral Beliefs about an Issue, When Do They Actually Disagree?

A challenge for relativists is to explain how two people can "disagree" in some sense if both of their apparently conflicting beliefs, say, about the permissibility of abortion, turn out to be correct or true. If it turns out, for example, that one person's moral dialect includes meaning and truth conditions for applying 'right action' that give high priority to reproductive rights and the other person's dialect gives high priority to preserving fetal life, then both parties might be saying true things when they express apparently incompatible positions. There is a pragmatic conflict here in the sense that their positions prescribe incompatible actions and social policies, but people may not see that conflict as solely pragmatic, but as a conflict over what is morally true.

The "may" is important. While critics of relativism (e.g., Bloomfield 2009) may presuppose that all laypeople (i.e., everyone who has not staked out a philosophical position on relativism) will treat the conflict as one over truth, this turns out to be false. The Goodwin and Darley study described earlier suggests that people can set aside the presumption that moral conflict is a disagreement over what is true or what is the single correct answer in the case of particularly intractable conflict. At the same time, the study suggests the need to explain the presumption. Analyses of the meaning and truth conditions of moral judgments can be more or less conducive to explaining this sort of mixed verdict from laypeople. For example, an "indexical" analysis of the meaning of moral judgments can make relativism too obvious as the metaethical view to have. The idea underlying an indexical analysis is that just as we know as part of the meaning of indexical terms that the reference of indexical terms is determined by certain contextual features of utterance – particularly the identity of the speaker or the near spatial environment of the speaker – so the truth conditions of moral judgments direct us to assess the judgment using the standards of the speaker. It is part of the meaning that the reference switches systematically according to the speaker. A competent user of an indexical, for example, knows that the reference and hence the truth conditions of "I" as in "I am a professor of philosophy" vary with the identity of the speaker. Very few competent users of moral language take it for granted that the truth conditions of moral judgments vary in this way.

"Truth relativists" offer a different approach to the semantic form of moral language based on the idea that some kinds of disagreements are "faultless": Two parties can genuinely disagree over a proposition and yet neither need be mistaken and both can be making true judgments. They stress that the disagreement is genuine because it is over the same proposition (thus departing from the indexical relativists) but that each party to the disagreement can be correctly assigning a different truth value to that proposition (see MacFarlane 2007; Kölbel 2013). This is possible because assignment of truth values can depend on a context of assessment usually set in connection with the person doing the assessing (perhaps the assessor's standards or sensibility). Truth relativists point to differences over taste to argue for the intuitive plausibility of faultless disagreements. Olivia believes that Matisse is better than Picasso, while Felicity believes that Picasso is better (Kölbel 2003). One might perceive genuine disagreement here, but also the possibility that Olivia and Felicity are applying different critical standards or have different aesthetic sensibilities for which neither can be faulted. When each makes a judgment, the truth of the proposition is set by her standards or sensibility, thus making for the possibility of different truth values. Truth relativism applied to a moral disagreement such as abortion might similarly hold that there is disagreement between those who affirm and those who deny the moral permissibility of abortion, but that the disagreement can be faultless because the truth values of the judgments will be set by the different standards of the assessors.

Significant numbers of the participants in the Goodwin and Darley study may indeed imply that the disagreement over abortion or stem-cell research is faultless, but it is not clear how truth relativism as applied to moral judgment explains the presumption, as earlier noted, that moral disagreements are conflicts over truth value. That is why participants are reluctant to assign a truth value to positions in such disagreements. The fact that the presumption can be overcome is not the same as there being a normal expectation that the truth value of moral judgments is set by a parameter determined by the assessor's standards.

We learn moral terms by learning criteria for their application from those who teach us the rest of our natural language. We are not taught that these criteria normally change with the speaker or assessor as a matter of the meaning or logic of the term. We initially are shown examples of right or wrong action, often our own actions or of those around us, and usually as part of our socialization. We are later given partial characterizations of such actions in more general terms describing, for instance, what kinds of actions are wrong. Most moral language users draw from exemplars (pointing to a particular case of someone's doing what they promised to do, even at some personal cost, for example) and partial characterizations (such as "Doing what you promised to do even at some personal cost") when they assign truth values to moral judgments (see Park 2022 for a clear analysis of how the meaning of moral concepts might be analyzed using the major theories of concepts in the literature).

Variation in the meaning and truth conditions of such judgments does not divide up according to tidy groups or societies or cultures. The processes by which moral languages, and the natural languages that contain them, come into being and evolve, exhibiting hybridity and incorporation of diverse influences, results in continual change and diversification in the meaning of terms. English originated as a German dialect that came to England through conquest by the Germanic Angles and Saxon tribes. It underwent subsequent transformations through invasions by Scandinavians and Normans. New languages emerge and evolve when different groups interact and migrate. Different groups who mingle through conquest or migration also mingle their norms and practices. Consider that national and regional differences between dialects of a natural language such as English can be substantial. Distinct regional dialects can evolve when English is learned by a group of people whose native language is other than English. The habits of their native language interact with and transform the vocabulary and grammar of the English that is transmitted to them. The interaction that takes place can give rise not only to different dialects, but also to different idiolects, as different speakers make individual accommodations in their vocabularies. There can be parallel processes in the evolution of moral languages.

Differences between dialects and idiolects may not be so apparent. Having a morality is usually a matter of holding plural values that are often in tension with each other, such as promoting good consequences and protecting individual rights, relationship and (personal) autonomy, or duties arising from special relationships and duties to one's fellow citizens or simply to human beings as such. Within a group of any size there can be differences in the way people resolve those tensions; differences in the priorities they tend to confer on this value when in conflict with that value. These differences may be stable enough to be embedded in criteria that individuals use to apply moral terms. Deep differences between the moral views of people in a group, society, or culture are very often interwoven with significant similarities, so that it is not obvious (though on the theory defended here, it turns out to be true) that there is enough variation in meaning and truth conditions to make for deep disagreements that are not conflicts over truth but only pragmatic conflicts.

Furthermore, if one has stereotypical views of the values of others who on some issues make significantly different moral judgments, of the nature that I characterized in Section 6 concerning the views of relationship-centered ethics, one is likely to dismiss their moral views as simply false, rather than seeing their views as being rooted in a tradition that supplies with respect to the relevant judgments significantly different content to the moral judgments that might come out true. This situation, it must be stressed, is not a matter of the adherents of relationship-centered ethics making certain judgments that are "true for them" but false for adherents of rights-centered ethics.

The case envisioned here is that the judgments of adherents of each tradition may turn out to be true, and in a way that *could be* recognized by adherents of the other tradition, once they recognize that in fact they mean different things with different truth conditions.

There is usually just enough in common between all the moral dialects and idiolects so as to foster uncertainty as to what the situation is. Going back to the Goodwin and Darley (2008), Wright et al. (2013) studies (see also Ayars and Nichols (2020), the result is a variety of metaethical views. Those who assume that moral disagreements are always disagreements in which the relevant moral concepts have the same content will tend to take universalist metaethical positions. Those who focus on the apparent intractability of some moral disagreements may conclude that in some ways, people are talking about different things and therefore may be inclined to reject universalism, at least for a certain class of moral disagreements. One theoretical advantage claimed for the pluralistic position defended here is that it makes possible a pretty good explanation for this diversity of metaethical viewpoints.

Are we all talking about the same thing, and is it just that some or all of us get off track and end up having false beliefs that create disagreement? Or is it that sometimes we are talking about the same thing, and our disagreements are over what is truly the case (because our moral concepts overlap in meaning and in the truth conditions for their application), and at other times we are not talking about the same thing, and our disagreements are not over what is true but are only pragmatic in nature (because the overlap in meaning and truth conditions is just that and not complete identity)? There may in fact be enough variation of all these kinds, and some people, reflecting on different bits of the evidence, can come to diverse metaethical conclusions (this explanation was advanced first, as far as I know, in Wong 2006 and elaborated in Wong 2011, 2014; but Olinder 2012 independently proposes another version of it).

14 Why We Have Different Beliefs in Metaethics

Philosophers, such as Michael Smith, often base a good part of their arguments for universalism on what they perceive to be laypeople's objectivist beliefs about morality and features of moral discourse, which those philosophers believe imply a belief in the objectivity of morals on the part of those laypeople. But these perceptions may reflect these philosophers' own presuppositions, which may not be shared by significant numbers of moral language users. Thus, if one holds that the semantic content of moral judgment refers to objective moral facts, or to moral properties that exist in the world completely independently of human thought and practice, this makes it difficult to explain why there are informed and intelligent moral language users, not just contrarian philosophers out to make a name for themselves, who are metaethical relativists.

On the other side, philosophers who defend metaethical relativism are often led to make claims about the content of moral judgment that makes it difficult for them to explain how competent moral language users could be anything other than metaethical relativists. If we accept Velleman's and Rovane's theories, then it becomes hard to explain why, unless they are very provincial, people don't recognize that they occupy moral worlds that are unintelligible to other people. If moral judgments refer to the implicit agreements to conduct oneself in certain ways on the condition that other parties to the agreement conduct themselves similarly (Harman 1975), then it becomes hard to explain why intelligent and informed moral language users don't recognize the possibility or reality of there being different moral communities based on different implicit agreements. If, with Dreier, we assume that we learn moral language by learning that the truth or falsity of a moral judgment depends on the speaker's moral commitments, again, it seems that we should all grow up to be metaethical relativists. And again, this makes puzzling the situation of varied metaethical belief as we find it.

A metaethical theory needs to explain why there are significant numbers of informed and intelligent people who are both universalists and relativists, and who aren't making some rather obvious mistake about the semantics of moral judgment and concepts. As argued in Section 7, some thoughtful and informed people have arrived at moral ambivalence. This too is not something obvious that any competent moral language user comes to accept in becoming a competent user. It comes from a commitment to serious inquiry into at least one serious rival to one's best interpretation of one's moral tradition. That commitment does not automatically result in moral ambivalence, but I have sketched one possible pathway in Section 7, starting with a contrast between relationship-centered ethics on the one hand, and rights-centered or utility-centered ethics on the other hand. I have sketched ways in which trying to go beyond the stereotypes that advocates of the latter two ethics might have of the former could lead to more serious consideration of relationship-centered ethics as a viable realization of a moral way of life.

More explicitly, the truth conditions of moral judgments can be set out in terms of reasons to be a person with certain kinds of traits or to perform certain actions. These could be reasons given a specified set of circumstances or conditions, or reasons all things considered. The truth conditions of moral judgments would specify the conditions under which we would have reason to address a person's suffering, to keep an agreement made, and so on.

The constraining effect of interpersonal and intrapersonal coordinating functions of morality together with common human motivational proclivities would make for significant overlap in reasons and thus the truth conditions for moral judgments, enough overlap such that those people who do not press inquiry into the areas of conflict over the specific conditions under which people hold there is reason to perform such actions could assume that the truth conditions are uniform. This way of viewing the semantics of moral judgments makes it no surprise that people could have different and conflicting metaethical views.

15 How Moral Reasons Enter into the Truth Conditions of Moral Judgments and Help Shape Our Moral Motivations

The final step of explanation is clarification of what form the truth conditions of moral judgments take. I have phrased the truth conditions in terms of the moral reasons that people have, where "moral" refers to the sort of normative guide that provides and sustains some structure to social cooperation and fosters internal motivational coherence within the individual. The feature of justifiability without coercion or deception is another feature of the conception of the moral employed here. But what is a reason? Some hold that whatever one has reason to do, moral or otherwise, must be based on the actual motivations, such as desires, that one has. That is, some hold that the relevant kind of reason has to be one capable of motivating a person to do what they have moral reason to do. However, this makes impossible what is one of the primary socializing functions of morality: to shape the motivations that people bring to social cooperation and thereby help them to lead their lives with a reasonable degree of internal motivational coherence. As indicated earlier, human beings inherit a diverse set of motivational inclinations: Some tend in the helpful, cooperative direction; others in the self-regarding direction; some are antagonistic toward at least some others. These unlearned dispositions are "raw" in the sense that they compete with one another for expression, and the conditions under which they become activated and express themselves can be pretty arbitrary in terms of consistency with moral values.

A child can find a baby bird fallen from a nest and instinctively seek to nurture it, but then turn around and ridicule a classmate for being overweight or speaking with a stutter. Learning what we have moral reason to do under which conditions is the way we train our premoral dispositions to become moral dispositions, or at least grow closer to them. If things go right from the moral point of view, the child learns to be compassionate more consistently and no longer seeks or even finds enjoyment or satisfaction in being cruel to a classmate.

To help us accomplish this, moral reasons must hold a prescriptive force that is independent of whatever premoral inclinations we begin with. This prescriptive force is similar to that of a command or advisory: The illocutionary force is that of a directive, but it is left open where the motivation to comply with it might come from. Part of it in most cases comes from unlearned dispositions of the individual as part of human adaptations for the cooperative life (I say in most cases, because of likely significant variability in unlearned dispositions among members of the human species, as there is in other biological species).

However, another part of the motivation may come from adaptations to follow what others do. This is part of how we are biologically fitted to receive the guidance of cultural norms. Tomasello (2019) has found in some of his studies that children, beginning around the age of three, have a readiness to follow whatever they have been taught as the rules for performing a certain kind of activity. For example, they insist on the proper way to perform a certain action in a game simply on the basis of having been shown that way to perform the action, even if that way has not been presented as *the* proper way to perform the action; the child will nevertheless protest if they see another player performing the activity in another way.

Moral socialization of unlearned dispositions occurs when these dispositions get engaged with teaching and modeling of norms that spell out the reasons to act in certain ways under certain conditions. The reasons guide and channel the dispositions and become part of the cognitive dimension of the corresponding emotion.[4] Compassion involves the perception of another being as suffering, and per the views of philosophers such as Mencius (*Mengzi*, 2006–2021, 3A5) and Martha Nussbaum (2001, 306) the perception of that being as not deserving that suffering. Mencius holds the plausible view that moral emotions involve affective, conative (motivating to action), and cognitive dimensions (see Wong 2015a, Wong 2015b for this interpretation). Natural compassion tends to be

---

[4] This means that a normative relativist cannot subscribe to the sort of metaethical relativism based on the idea that all moral reasons that people have are motivating reasons – based on desire or motivational propensity present in their motivational systems. Gilbert Harman (1975) is the foremost proponent of this kind of metaethical relativism. For a criticism of this view, see Wong (2006, 74–75). One of the most debatable assumptions Harman makes is that morality is founded upon implicit agreements that people make with one another in structuring their social cooperation. As argued earlier, this runs into the heterogeneity of people's moral commitments even though they cooperate with one another in various ways and make moral judgments about each other. It also runs against the conception of morality as a part of culture that shapes human motivation and is not simply responsive to it. On the viewpoint defended here, moral reasons are not internal to the motivations human beings already have. On the other hand, neither do they have motivational force on their own. When they do succeed in motivating, they engage with one or more of the motivations mentioned in this section.

erratically expressed: not always present when it should be, and sometimes prompting conduct that is inappropriate to the circumstances or no conduct at all when doing something is in order. When it becomes a moral virtue, compassion is guided by a reliable sense of when one has reason to respond to the suffering of others. The moral development of this emotion involves an interaction between its different dimensions: The apprehension of moral reasons channels the affective and conative tendencies toward appropriate expression. On the other side of this interaction, the affective and conative tendencies provide motivational efficacy to the reasons that channel and guide them.

This conception of moral cultivation, in which the cognitive, affective, and conative interact and reinforce one another, finds analogy in the contemporary psychologist Martin Hoffman's work (2000) on the role of empathy in moral development. Hoffman has suggested that a child begins to internalize morality when they experience empathic distress upon witnessing another person's distress. The earliest modes of empathic arousal are primitive, automatic, and involuntary processes. Hoffman thinks that the most effective child-rearing takes advantage of occasions when primitive empathy is aroused and used in moral teaching. A child hurts another, for example, and an adult might arouse empathy in the perpetrator by pointing out the effect on the victim, expressing disapproval, and suggesting apology or reparation.

When such a sequence is repeated many times, "scripts" are created and encoded in memory so that they influence later decisions and behavior. It is important that the kind of induction that presents moral reasons to the child be given in an emotionally evocative situation so that the cognition of what the child is being taught can be made "hot" by the activation of affective and motivational proclivities and through the linking of the proclivities to the reasons. Hoffman goes on to suggest that moral norms or principles can acquire their motivational efficacy through association with activated affective and motivational proclivities. At the same time, the norms or principles, through getting linked to the proclivities, can correct certain biases that accompany the untutored proclivities, such as the greater tendency to ignore the distress of those persons who are unfamiliar to us or to forget the distress of those who are not present to us here and now (I discuss the relationship between Mencius and Hoffman in Wong 2015a and 2015b).

The anthropologist Naomi Quinn (2005) identifies one cross-cultural universal of child-rearing as the linking of moral lessons with emotional arousal, so as to make the lessons unmistakable, memorable, and motivating. In her discussion of Chinese child-rearing, for example, Quinn identifies the practice of shaming as an instrument for bringing home a moral lesson to a child while emotionally arousing them. Quinn points out that moral lessons are a pervasive and consistent feature of social life for a child, often not explicitly stated, but communicated by adults in a glance, a gesture, a posture, and even in what is not said. She further suggests some neurological correlates of these universal features. The regularity of lesson-giving strengthens certain synaptic connections in the brain; and drawing from Joseph LeDoux's work (2002, 200–234), Quinn points out that hormones released during emotional arousal actually strengthen synaptic connections and organize and coordinate brain activity, crowding out all but the emotionally relevant experience from consciousness. One might surmise that constancy of lesson-giving, woven into the fabric of everyday life, strengthens these synaptic connections even more. This kind of moral socialization is what gives moral reasons their motivational efficacy, and to do this they cannot simply be based on what a person is already motivated to do, but must be capable of engaging and guiding motivations that may only be incipient.

16 Summary of the Argument for a Pluralistic Form of Metaethical Moral Relativism

This completes the sketch of a naturalistic conception of morality that begins with recognition of cultural norms that have functions of promoting and sustaining interpersonal cooperation and intrapersonal coherence of motivation. There are universal constraints on how these functions could be adequately fulfilled, given characteristic human motivations and ends. However, these constraints cannot narrow down the range of moralities that fulfill the functions of morality to just one. More specific normative guidance is given through the way that the plurality of values in a morality are handled when they come into conflict. In Section 6, we got an example of differences between more specific action-guiding moralities in the way that certain kinds of conflicts between values of relationship and autonomy might be handled in moralities that are more relationship-centered versus moralities that are more personal-autonomy-centered. Understanding how these conflicts might be best handled within these morality types produces in some of us the sense of moral ambivalence: the sense of significant uncertainty as to whether there is a singular truth as to how to balance or prioritize values that are shared across different moral traditions.

A naturalistic conception of morality that draws from the human sciences is then put forward to explain why we might arrive at moral ambivalence. Morality, it is proposed, is a normative guide that emerges from human culture to foster and regulate social cooperation and coherence between diverse and potentially conflicting motivations within the individual. Moral enculturation shapes us in accordance with certain ideals of the kinds of persons we ought to be.

These ideals are specified in terms of reasons to be and to act in certain ways. Because cooperation requires some substantial degree of agreement on these ideals and norms, we tend to think of morality as something shared with others, and that enables us to form expectations that we can ask them to justify their actions and ways of being toward us. However, there is no pregiven Platonic heaven of moral values that constitutes the singularly true justifications that we should be giving to each other. In presenting to others our conceptions of what we have moral reasons to be and to do, we are not getting at a pre-existing moral fabric of the universe. We are weaving a human fabric through contending, accommodating, and working with one another.

What is universal takes shape in the intersection between the functions of morality and the types of animals we tend to be, with unlearned motivations given through natural selection. Though these motivations can undergo considerable shaping through moral and other kinds of socialization, they do place certain limits on what an adequate morality that fulfills its functions could broadly look like. Within these limits, there is no one true morality, and this makes it possible to experience moral ambivalence. Unlike other ways of arriving at metaethical moral relativism, this picture of how we arrive at a plurality of true and most justified moralities does not give us any reason to expect that either philosophers or laypeople would ordinarily arrive at simple versions of either relativism or universalism. If the semantics of moral judgment leaves open the question of whether there is a single true morality, and if we both substantially converge on some kinds of moral issues because of the universal constraints and substantially diverge on other kinds, we get what the picture advocated in this Element predicts. This metaethical pluralism seems to be what empirical study has found among laypeople, and the pluralism certainly exists among philosophers.

Sections 1–7 discussed the way that normative concerns can and should guide our *inquiry* into the question of metaethical moral relativism. The final Sections of this Element return to normative issues and discusses *how one should act toward others if one has accepted pluralistic metaethical moral relativism*. The view in question is often called normative moral relativism.

17 Confused Reasoning That Is Sometimes Attributed to Those Who Believe in Normative Moral Relativism

"Normative moral relativism" is often associated with the view that one ought to tolerate people who act on different moral beliefs than one's own, or that one ought not to impose one's beliefs on those with different beliefs, letting them live by their beliefs, or that one ought to treat them in accordance with the standards they apply to themselves. Such normative views are in turn often inferred from metaethical relativism. The thought here is that if there is no single true morality, then one would be right to adopt a "hands-off" stance. Such an inference has been criticized as invalid. Harrison (1976) argues that metaethical relativism is a claim made from an "external" viewpoint outside any moral system of values and rules, while a requirement to be tolerant is made from within a moral system. The former cannot support the latter. Bernard Williams (1981) points out that the normative views seem to be applied universally to everyone, and based on a universal normative principle requiring toleration. If indeed metaethical moral relativism were the view that there were no moral values or norms that applied to everyone, to espouse on its basis a universal policy of toleration would be self-contradictory.

However, there are alternative ways to construe metaethical moral relativism and its relationship to normative moral relativism. Normative moral relativists should grant that it is a nonstarter to try to derive a normative requirement to be tolerant solely from a metaethical claim. The normative requirement need not be derived from metaethical moral relativism alone. Recall that in Sections 4 and 5, the argument for extended inquiry into the moral traditions of others was of two types: the first was based on a conception of epistemic rationality and addressed to all; the second was addressed toward those with certain moral values such as respect for others, at least to the extent that one is ready to regard as wrong distorting or simplifying their moral traditions for the sake of calling them inferior people or viewing them as having inferior cultures and justifying conduct toward them that otherwise would be unjust, oppressive, and exploitative. The second line of argument for *extended inquiry* can be extended to apply to *conduct* toward those who may be living according to moralities different from one's own, but which are as true or as justified as one's own.

18 An Argument for Normative Moral Relativism That Is Contingent upon the Acceptance of Certain Values and the Adoption of Metaethical Moral Relativism

Suppose you value respect for the autonomy of individuals and of peoples. Arguably, to treat individuals as Kantian ends in themselves is to respect value commitments they have made that cannot be criticized as rationally mistaken or false. What does it mean to respect their autonomy? Arguably, one meaning is to refrain from interfering with their actions in ways that cannot be rationally justified to them. Let's call this "justifiability autonomy." Unlike Kant, normative moral relativists do not assume that regarding respect for autonomy as a universal value binding on everyone is necessary to regard it as binding on oneself.

They rather might be addressing all those who do have such a value, and perhaps those who might be persuaded to adopt it based on other related values they hold, and are applying that value in conjunction with a belief in the existence of apparently rationally irresolvable moral disagreements (Wong 1984). The inference is made from both metaethical relativism *and* a certain value that they may hold as moral agents.

19 Why Normative Moral Relativism Cannot Be a Simple Matter of Letting Others Be

This argument for normative moral relativism is coherent, but being coherent does not prevent complications, any more than it does for any other moral view. As pointed out in Section 12, the others with whom we disagree probably do not constitute a cohesive and uniform group. They are diverse and disagree with each other, as well as with ourselves. Recognizing this more complex situation requires moral relativists, normative or metaethical, to depart from an assumption they sometimes make – that there are relatively uniform and cohesive moral communities that disagree externally with other communities but not internally. But as argued in Sections 13–15, this is not at all a necessary consequence or ground for holding that there is no single true morality (see also Wong 2011). The normative upshot is that it is rarely so neat a matter of our getting to decide whether or not to let "others" alone. Some of those others may prefer that we intervene on their side, and others will not. And yet, both sides may be so interdependent on each other that there is little hope of being able to say, "Well, let's not interfere with those others, but support the ones who agree with us."

Further complications arise on our own side. We find reason not to interfere with others on the basis of our value of justifiability autonomy. But this kind of autonomy is not the only value that we hold. In case a disagreement involves these other values, normative relativists have a reason to act on these values, even if the opposing side cannot be criticized as rationally mistaken or as holding false beliefs. In other words, the value of justifiability autonomy provides a reason for toleration or lettings others be, but that reason need not be regarded as overriding the reasons provided by every other moral value held by normative relativists. If normative relativists hold plural moral values, then values other than justifiability autonomy, such as the defense of innocent life, might provide reasons to severely condemn and interfere with the practices of others even if there is no rational refutation of these practices available. Why? Subscribing to a value is a matter not only of holding oneself to it, but of seeking to have it realized in the world, which means trying to get others to live by it. As argued in Sections 14–15, subscribing to a value does not mean presupposing that everyone has a motivating reason to act on it. The upshot is that normative relativists might have to decide which of their own values they give priority to in the case at hand, or they might try to devise a course of action that would allow them to act on all the relevant values at stake. In this respect, normative relativists would not be much different from other moral agents who hold a plurality of values that sometimes come into conflict given a certain set of circumstances. To illustrate this point, I shall discuss the practice of female genital cutting. This case also illustrates the way that inadequate inquiry into the moral traditions underlying this practice can be a failure of epistemic rationality, and also an example of the way that sweeping condemnations of the varied practices falling under "female genital cutting" can be a violation of justifiability autonomy. A better approach may, it will be argued, involve application of the value of accommodation.

20 What Is Female Genital Cutting?

Even the name "female genital cutting" raises normative controversy. Most critics of this practice call it "female genital mutilation" and would complain that mere "cutting" grossly underplays the brutality of the practice. Here, the choice is to use the word "cutting," which is usually adopted to convey the wide variation in what is done: Forms of this practice vary significantly, from a pricking of the genitalia to draw a drop of blood, to removal of the hood of the clitoris, to removal of the entire external clitoris, to removal of all external genitalia with stitching together of the resulting wound. The persons on whom it is practiced range from infants to adult women who consent to it. The great majority of those who arrange and perform the practice are women. Where there is female genital cutting, there is almost always a corresponding practice for males. Surveys in Africa reveal that when compared with men, an equal or higher proportion of women favor continuation of female genital cutting (Public Policy Advisory Network on Female Genital Surgeries in Africa 2012, 23). The practice is sometimes endorsed and performed by women (over objections to its acceptability from the majority of men), and sometimes initiated and performed by teenage girls (over the objections to its acceptability by the entire adult community; Thomas 1996; Leonard 2000; both cited by Earp 2016, 112). Which forms of the practice are prevalent depends on the region and which group engages in it. For example, "type III" or "infibulation" (removal of the external genitalia and the suturing of the vulva) is much more prevalent in Djibouti, Egypt, Eritrea, Somalia, and Sudan than in other countries (Yoder et al. 2013, 202). These constitute 10 percent of cases in Africa. The remaining cases are type I (reduction of the clitoral hood or the external elements of clitoral tissue), and type II (partial or complete labial reductions and partial or complete reductions of the external elements of clitoral tissue) (Public Policy Advisory Network on Female Genital Surgeries in Africa 2012, 22).

The rationales for the practice also vary widely: Control of female sexuality is often featured in criticism of the practice, but reasons given by its adherents include their viewing it as a rite of passage and test of courage, establishment of a gender identity, entrance into a secret society, resistance to colonialism and postcolonial Western domination, and a generalized adherence to tradition (Kratz 2002; Lyons 2007; Shweder 2003). Sometimes a religious rationale is given. Muslims who engage in the practice often cite portions of the Hadith, the sayings and deeds attributed to the Prophet Mohammed. There are alternative interpretations of the relevant sayings. Some dispute their authenticity and seek to decouple female genital cutting from Islamic approval. Other interpretations argue that according to one saying in particular the Prophet Mohammed posed limitations on the practice of female genital cutting that predated Islam, enjoining practitioners not to cut severely and thereby destroy genital tissue (Duivenbode and Padela 2019, 287, 290).

Since opponents of female genital cutting often assume that the practice functions to control female sexuality, it is worthwhile to point out the evidence against this assumption. Almost all societies that practice female genital cutting also practice male genital cutting, and the reasons given for it are often similar. In some cultures, the rite for girls elevates their social status, promotes within-sex bonding, and provides increased personal and political agency. In cultures where there is only a rite for boys, the lack of one for girls reflects their lower status (Earp and Johnsdotter 2021; Gruenbaum et al. 2022).

The World Health Organization (2008), an agency of the United Nations, has taken the position that "female genital mutilation" is morally wrong in all its forms. Earp points out that while some types of the practice result in extreme pain and profound trauma (2016, 127), and that these types may be impermissible regardless of cultural context and in particular if carried out on children, the same cannot be said of some other types. Some of the rationales for especially the most radical forms of the practice might not pass the constraint of justifiability to the governed. On the other side, it is pointed out that the meaning of pain varies with cultural context. Sometimes women undergoing the practice reject the use of anesthesia and emphasize the importance of preparing for the pain of childbirth and of demonstrating maturity (Shell-Duncan and Hernlund 2000, 16; cited by Earp 2016, 127). Lyons (2007) notes that most Westerners react much less negatively to painful initiation rites undergone by males because of a gendered difference in expectations. Nelson Mandela recounts his own ritual circumcision, performed without anesthesia, the agonizing pain of which was expected to be suffered in silence as a test of courage (Mandela 2006).

Fuambai Ahmadu, an anthropologist born in Sierra Leone but raised in the United States, returned to her country of birth to undergo the cutting by the Bondo women's secret society in her Kono tribe. She disputes the claim that the practice diminishes sexual pleasure for women, arguing that the criticism presupposes an excessively mechanical picture of sexuality, omitting the role of the mind as the most important sexual organ (research by gynecologists and others have confirmed women who have undergone the procedure have rich sexual lives, including desire, arousal, orgasm, and satisfaction; see Public Policy Advisory Network on Female Genital Surgeries in Africa 2012, 22). Even if just the mechanical picture is considered, the traditional form of the procedure does not remove most of the clitoris, nor does it remove the tissue and structures necessary for orgasm (Catania et al. 2007; Ahmadu and Shweder 2009; Abdulcadir et al. 2016). Ahmadu found among the Kono no cultural obsession with feminine chastity, virginity, or sexual fidelity. The role of the father is considered marginal to the central "matricentric unity" (Ahmadu 2001, 285).

This is not to deny that there are forms of the practice that fit the vehement criticisms usually launched against it in the West and in the countries in which they originate. What is brought home, however, is the need for more serious and tempered reconsideration of the broadsides leveled against female genital cutting. Such generalizations can backfire by angering those who feel judged but not respected enough to be heard. It leaves critics open to the counter-criticism that there is more fair comparison than they are willing to acknowledge between some forms of female genital cutting on the one hand, and on the other hand, male circumcision and female cosmetic genital surgery, which are taken for granted and accepted in the West (Boddy 2016, 2020). It also raises the question of whether the disposition of many in the Western philosophical, ethical, and political traditions to regard themselves as having discovered the true forms of universality fosters a careless disregard for practices it is inclined to dismiss as barbaric, to the extent that it overlooks important differences among these practices and among the rationales given by their adherents. It raises the question of whether this disposition is unwittingly inherited from the long history of powerful societies rationalizing acts of colonialism, oppression, and exploitation through characterization of others or their cultures as inferior (see Gruenbaum 2001; Njambi 2004, 2011; Boddy 2007; Oba 2008).

The form of cutting that consists only in pricking has increased in acceptance as sufficient among immigrants to the West from countries in which more severe forms of the practice have been customary. When Somali immigrant mothers requested of a Seattle, Washington hospital to have both their boys and girls circumcised, and when the medical staff learned that most of these mothers had undergone infibulations, the staff could not contemplate performing the procedure. However, the doctor chairing the committee charged to address the question felt it a necessary expression of respect that they try to understand how Somali parents viewed female genital cutting. Discussions led some Somali parents to propose the compromise of a nick to the hood over the clitoris that would draw blood. That proposal received support within the hospital, partly on the grounds that some parents said that if denied the moderate procedure they might take their daughters out of the country to get the more radical procedure done. The compromise fell by the wayside when the matter exploded into heated moral and political controversy, as some termed all forms of female genital cutting "barbaric," while in contrast one obstetrician-gynecologist at the hospital countered that the nicking of the prepuce was a good deal less drastic than what is done to boys when they are circumcised (Ostrom 1996). In light of such ethical considerations, the anthropologist Richard Shweder has proposed that liberal, pluralistic societies should try to accommodate groups desiring to engage in the practice on two conditions: first, that only moderate procedures should be performed on those below the age of consent (no major irreversible alterations of the body); and second, that those who have reached the age of consent should have the right to alter their bodies in substantial ways (Shweder 2003, 206; see also Shweder 2022; Earp 2022).

Thus, normative moral relativism need not endorse a simplistic and categorical letting others be; it can legitimately matter to us when others violate our values, and the justifiability autonomy of others is not necessarily the final word. Normative relativism can take the form of a type of moral consideration for nonintervention or tolerance, but it need not take the form of the prescriptive final word. However, if we contemplate condemning, intervening, or prohibiting, we should undertake a serious inquiry as to the extent and manner to which others actually do violate our values, and why. We may find that the practices in question and the rationales for them depart from our stereotypes of them, and we may have to face our own hypocrisies and inconsistencies, or we may find ourselves unable to justify the rational superiority of our judgments over theirs. That should matter to us, and we may find reason either to straightforwardly accept the practices or to try to find compromise.

Recall that the sort of metaethical moral relativism defended in this Element is distinguished by universal constraints on the range of true moralities. Not all moralities are true, but a range of moralities can be true. One of the constraints is that all true moralities must contain the value of accommodation. The most general characterization of this value is a willingness to maintain constructive relationship with others with whom one is in serious and even intractable disagreement.

The rationale is based on the function of morality of promoting and sustaining social cooperation: Such cooperation would come under impossible pressure if it always depended on strict agreement; hence human beings must at least sometimes be willing to cooperate even though they disagree about important matters.

One example of an act of accommodation is the Seattle hospital's offer (before it had to be retracted) to perform the moderate procedure. On the one hand, the Seattle hospital had to avoid doing harm to any of its patients, even at the behest of the patients' families. On the other hand, it had adopted the value of welcoming and serving people of all cultural, racial, and ethnic backgrounds, and of adapting its treatment of patients in accordance with these backgrounds, subject to constraints deriving from other considerations such as the avoidance of doing harm. Trying to satisfy both constraints led to the compromise proposal. The harm is arguably minimal, and the offer accommodated those Somali parents who were willing to accept the proposed procedure more for its ritual-like aspects than for any permanent alteration effected. While it may not have satisfied parents who desired such a permanent alteration, it was responsive to those who said that if they were not given the compromise option, they would have the procedure performed on their daughters elsewhere, and if so, the procedure would involve major and permanent alteration.

21 Accommodation and the Fraught Issue of Abortion

Another possible case where the value of accommodation might be especially relevant is the disagreement over abortion, which has been heightened with the Supreme Court having struck down *Roe* v. *Wade* in *Dobbs* v. *Jackson Women's Health Organization* (2022). In *Roe*, the Court ruled that there was a constitutional right to choose abortion, the scope of which depended on the stage of pregnancy (the fewest restrictions by the state are imposed on the right during the first trimester; during the second trimester, the state may regulate abortion in ways that are reasonably related to maternal health; and during the third trimester the state can regulate or prohibit abortion in the interests of protecting prenatal life, with exceptions to the prohibition for the sake of protecting maternal life or health; *Roe* v. *Wade* 1973, 410 U.S. 113). *Planned Parenthood v. Casey* (1992) affirmed a constitutional right to abortion during the first trimester but gave states more scope to restrict abortions. *Dobbs* v. *Jackson Women's Health Organization* (2022) overruled both previous decisions of the Court, holding that there was no constitutional right to abortion and returning the authority to regulate abortion to the states.

The legal scholar Jamal Greene (2021) has argued that the rancorous debate over abortion in the public sphere shows how divisive is the conception of rights that has come to dominate American legal culture and perhaps the culture at large. The conception of rights as "presumptively absolute, yielding only in special circumstances, if at all" (Greene 2021, 7), is divisive in its effects because it ensures that there must be winners and losers in the adjudication of what rights there are and who possesses them. Another formulation of this conception of rights is that they protect interests that "trump" competing interests and cannot be balanced against the public good (Dworkin 1977). Greene tends to present *Roe* as applying the conception of rights as trumps because it recognizes a right to abortion but none for the fetus.

Perhaps a fairer and more sympathetic reading of *Roe* and its fate may conclude that its attempt to navigate *between* contending absolutes fell victim to the mentality of rights as absolute trumps. *Roe*, and even more so, *Casey*, does not affirm an unconditional right to have an abortion. In *Roe*, the scope of the right is limited by the stage of pregnancy and the type of reason that might be given for abortion. The test for permissible restriction during the first trimester is "strict scrutiny": restriction must be narrowly tailored to meet a compelling state interest, using the least restrictive means to achieve that interest. It is this relatively strong right during the first trimester that prompts Greene to say that *Roe* implied an "absolute right to a first-trimester abortion" (2021, 128). However, this absoluteness disappears with the second and third trimesters.

The litigating sides in *Roe* actually have a better claim to have staked truly absolute positions. The state of Texas argued that the fetus is a person protected by the 14th amendment and that protecting prenatal life is a compelling state interest. Jane Roe and others involved argued that Texas invaded the individual's right to liberty under the 14th amendment, and that the right to an abortion is absolute; that a person is entitled to end pregnancy at any time, for any reason, and in any way. The majority opinion, written by Harry Blackmun, actually steered between these absolutes, holding that states have rights to protect potential human life after the point of viability, identifying that point as occurring during the third trimester of pregnancy. This, along with authority to regulate abortion in ways reasonably related to the health of the pregnant person (activated during the second trimester), substantially limits the right to have an abortion. *Casey* changed the trimester framework of *Roe* in favor of making the point of fetal viability the threshold for state interest in protecting prenatal life, noting that that point of viability changed with advances in medical technology. It furthermore raised the standard for deciding when a restriction on abortion is invalid: It must impose an "undue burden" on the person having the right, or a substantial obstacle in that person's path.

It may be, as Greene suggests, that *Roe*'s omission of a right of the fetus to life enraged and triggered the radicalization of the pro-life movement. In any case, there emerged a concerted and ultimately successful attempt to change the composition of the Supreme Court to a majority willing to strike down *Roe* and *Casey*. Their demise puts the question of the legal regulation of abortion in the hands of the states. At the time of this writing, the various states display a wide regulatory range, from outright bans from conception onward; to recognizing a right to abortion until the fetus is viable, or if necessary to protect the life and health of the mother; to allowing abortions throughout pregnancy (World Population Review 2022). The state legislative response to *Dobbs* conveys a picture of a country splintering along political, cultural, and moral seams, marked by violent, often abusive, and contemptuous discourse, punctuated by awful physical violence and intimidating threats screamed out over social media.

Greene suggests that the "trumping" conception of rights contributed to this situation. He proposes a different conception that treats rights in general as inherently limited but allows that in exceptional circumstances some rights could be treated as nearly absolute. One set of exceptional circumstances is exemplified by the US history of racial discrimination, segregation, and systematic, intentional subjugation of groups. When the state engages in these acts, a proper response is the assertion of the relevant rights as trumps. However, treating all rights in this way results in existential battles over who has which rights. The conception Greene advocates, that of rights as inherently limited, is consistent with an approach called "proportionality," which is dominant across legal systems in the world except for the United States. Proportionality is consistent with recognizing many, varied kinds of rights which need to be balanced against each other and against governmental and social interests. "Structured proportionality" is constituted by a multistage process whereby distinct questions must be answered in the right ways to advance to the next stage of adjudicating proposed restrictions of rights in favor of other rights or interests: Does the proposed restriction pursue a legitimate goal? Is the restriction a suitable means of pursuing the goal? Is there a less intrusive but equally effective means? Is the restriction justified (proportionate) in light of the gain in the protection for the competing right or interest (see Möeller 2012)?

Greene points to Germany's treatment of abortion as an example of what the alternative might encourage, both in terms of a less contentious way to deal with disagreements over when abortions should be allowed and in terms of a conception of rights as inherently limited and in need of balancing in cases of conflict. Its treatment is more consonant with the fact that the best way to protect fetal life is not to outlaw abortion (which only drives the practice underground)

but rather to provide pregnant persons with meaningful alternatives to termination. German courts have structured abortion jurisprudence around both the
rights of the pregnant person and the fetus. Abortion is technically illegal but
can be performed without prosecution during the first twelve weeks of pregnancy
with mandatory counseling and a three-day waiting period, or (beyond the first
twelve weeks) for reasons relating to significant threats to the pregnant person's
health or life, serious genetic irregularities of the fetus, or severe emotional
distress or unusual hardships associated with pregnancy or childbirth, and in
cases of pregnancies resulting from rape or incest. Further, the state must provide
prenatal care, childcare, and employment guarantees that encourage women to
choose to give birth. Greene asserts that although German courts started from
a premise of fetal rights, today it is easier (and often much cheaper) to obtain
abortions in Germany than in much of the United States. In the United States, "A
more accommodating judicial strategy might have brought the two sides closer
together, and perhaps even better protected women, in this most divisive of
political conflicts," he writes (Greene 2021, 90).

However, cultural differences and political structures vary across Germany
and the United States, and it would be very difficult to securely establish
counterfactuals. A conception of rights, even one that has become dominant
in a country's jurisprudence, does not by itself determine *how* specific issues
involving rights will be adjudicated. Canadian jurisprudence also tries to balance rights by deploying a test of structured proportionality. But Canada has no
criminal restrictions on abortion whatsoever. The Canadian Supreme Court
(*R.* v. *Morgentaler* 1988) struck down a law that had criminalized the performance of abortions except in cases where hospital committed provided certifica-
tion that continuation of the pregnancy would or would likely endanger the
pregnant person's life or health. However, it did not establish a constitutional
right to abortion. There were three separate opinions presented in support of the
majority's decision. All three opinions agreed that the abortion law violated the
pregnant person's right to security, but they did so on the grounds that access to
the hospital committee was not equally available across the country and that the
legally required procedure could result in extensive delays which could further
endanger the pregnant person's life or health. Further, the Court was unanimous
in holding that the state had a legitimate interest in protection of the fetus. But
regulation was left up to the legislature, which has not passed a law on abortion
since. After *Dobbs*, there was a call in Canada from some quarters to pre-
emptively establish a legal right to abortion, but a number of abortion rights
advocates cautioned against the move, fearing that it would provoke anti-choice
legislators to retract it when they were in the majority. This complex story, when
put alongside Germany's, does not offer assurance that having a conception of

rights more amenable to their being balanced against each other or other interests is going to by itself bring about a less fraught and contentious disagreement over abortion.

Such a conception of rights might facilitate the kind of negotiation between different moral viewpoints in a pluralistic society that Greene is calling for, but it is hardly sufficient. A broader sort of social and political change would need to take place that gives people space to deal with the moral complexity of their own positions and those of others. They would need to encounter others with substantially different views, and in contexts that provide them a better sense of the full humanity of these others. The effect of closer encounters with others would be something like the effect I am striving to produce through this Element: prompting deeper exploration of what lies behind and belies the stereotypes we have of others. This will help in the kind of effort necessary for those who seek sufficient consensus on a reasonable and humane solution to the abortion disagreement. Though national legislation is a possible solution, liberals will likely have to engage in retail politics on the state and local levels with people who have somewhat different views than they have. They will have to accommodate, but to do that, they will have to know how they can connect with others who disagree, not so as to eliminate disagreement, but to work with them on some things that both sides want.

22 Undermining Stereotypes of the Other Side

To portray the conflict as one between hardened sides that each champion their one true answer is to mischaracterize the moral thinking and feeling of the vast majority of Americans. In a recent study (Bruce 2020), sociologists conducted in-depth interviews with people who were given the time to qualify, explain, and state "on the one hand" and "on the other hand." Most do not take categorical positions either for or against abortion rights.[5] They neither hold that a woman's right to abortion nor that the life of the fetus is the only relevant moral consideration. This already is to depart from the characteristic public debate on the issue, which features one consideration but not the other, as if it did not exist.

Considerable numbers of those in the middle couched their positions as generally permitting abortion but not under some conditions, most frequently in the later stages of pregnancy or after viability, or sometimes if the behavior leading to pregnancy had shown carelessness or irresponsibility toward birth

---

[5] They conducted 217 in-depth interviews in California, Colorado, Indiana, North Dakota, Pennsylvania, and Tennessee in 2019. The sample approximated diversity (in political ideology, religious preference, religious attendance, race, age, marital status, children or no children, political affiliation) across the US adult population overall.

control. Other considerable numbers of those in the middle couched their positions as generally opposing abortion but permitting it under some conditions, most often when the woman's life was in danger, pregnancy had been caused by rape, incest, or domestic abuse, when at the earlier stages of pregnancy or before viability, and in cases of financial and psychological unreadiness to care for a child. There are also considerable numbers of people who can't be categorized as being generally for or against, with excepting conditions. Some say the morality of abortion has to be judged on a case-by-case basis. Others say that they would not judge the decisions of others on abortion, sometimes because they accept a plurality of moral positions on abortion; sometimes because they have not been in the situation of having to make the decision for themselves and therefore feel unqualified to judge others in that situation; sometimes because they *have* been in that situation and resist categorical judgment about what they did; and sometimes because they consider that it "depends on the person" and their situation in a way that makes it inappropriate for others to judge.

In another study, an overwhelming majority of US-resident adults expressed willingness to help a close friend or family member seeking abortion. Not surprisingly, those who regard abortion to be immoral were willing to offer the fewest forms of support and at the lowest level. Yet almost half in this group would help a friend or family member with arrangements, and over a third would help with associated costs. A majority who think the morality of abortion depends on certain factors would offer logistical help and with the associated costs of abortion (Cowan et al. 2022, 4). Reasons given in interviews for this "discordant benevolence" indicate both differing values and shared values. One reason is "commiseration." Some would help a friend or family member because they view them as a human worthy of care, despite their moral disapproval of the choice that person is making. A conservative Republican who had had her own abortion but thinks of the procedure as killing would still support another woman in a similar situation because "we make bad choices, but we're still good people." A liberal Democrat who got pregnant when single and was scared because she "didn't have anybody" morally opposes abortion. Nevertheless, she would say to others considering abortion: "I'm here for you ... I'm here no matter what," because "everybody needs somebody to help them through it" (Cowan et al. 2022, 6).

Cowan and her colleagues call a second reason for discordant benevolence "exemption" because it "carves out a condition of exceptionality to help reserved exclusively for their friend(s) or family member(s)." That is, abortion is regarded as morally unacceptable but an exception in terms of helping it take place is made in affirming the value of helping close others in need. Ryan, a liberal Democrat who opposes abortion on the grounds of taking responsibility for life, would be willing to help his sister have an abortion if she was set on it, though he would not help her pay for it (Cowan et al. 2022, 7). A third reason for discordant benevolence is "discretion." At the same time that one can think that it is morally wrong to have an abortion, one can also hold that it is the individual's right to make their own decision (Cowan et al. 2022, 8). It would have been interesting to know more about the scope of this kind of "moral individualism," as Cowan and her colleagues call it (2022, 7). It seems implausible that people would apply it to just any moral view that was at odds with their own. A possible explanation is that people give more weight to letting others make their own decisions when the moral issue is one that is particularly difficult to view as having only one right solution. Abortion is a position on which people do hold moral positions, even strongly held and felt positions, but on which they also recognize that informed people of good faith hold different positions.

The acts that the study of Cowans and her colleagues describe are acts of accommodation. Going forward, it might be hoped that pro-life advocates would recognize the most effective way to reduce abortion is to make it more financially and emotionally feasible to carry a pregnancy to term, and that pro-choice advocates would approve of making more feasible the choice to have a child as well as the choice to abort. People can operate from a definite moral point of view on abortion but recognize the complexity of the issue and their own values and choose a way of acting on their point of view and their other values that reflects a degree of moral ambivalence.

23 Fostering Pluralistic Encounters

Put in its most general form, is it possible to foster, and even to institutionalize, the idea of people coming together to explore how they might deal with their moral differences and find ways to accommodate each other? The moral-political climate in the United States at the time of this writing presents a daunting challenge, but efforts to bring people of different backgrounds together to deliberate upon what divides us show promise and some results.

A type of study made up of a series of experiments and known as "deliberative polling" brings together people of diverse backgrounds to discuss and make recommendations on issues many of which provoke vehement and entrenched disagreement, such as energy policy, immigration, and what to do about crime. The political scientist James Fishkin (2009) conceived of events in which citizens convened, typically for a weekend, to deliberate over such issues. They were chosen on the basis of random representative samplings and were supplied with briefing materials on the issues, attended talks given by experts, and part of the time met in small discussion groups led by trained moderators. They were polled for their views at the beginning and at the end, and the results typically showed significant change. A concrete example of when such events had significant impact is the deliberative polling done in the American state of Texas on the issue of energy policy. This produced significant shifts in citizens' opinions on the viability of wind power, resulting in Texas utilities and governmental regulars investing in that technology (Galbraith and Price 2013).

Another of the more intriguing ideas for getting more input from more parts of the body politic is that of

> an "open mini-public": a large, all-purpose, randomly selected assembly of between 150 and 1,000 people from diverse backgrounds, gathered for an extended period of time (from at least a few days to a few years) for the purpose of agenda-setting and law-making of some kind, and connected via crowdsourcing platforms and deliberative forums (including other mini-publics) to the larger population. (Landemore 2020, 13)

A striking realization of a deliberative mini-public is the Irish Citizens Assembly, whose work resulted in the adoption of groundbreaking laws on abortion and marriage equality (see Farrell et al. 2019). People asked to participate agreed to meet on weekends to receive information from experts chosen across the political spectrum, and the information was also made available to the public.

Throughout the twentieth century, Ireland, an overwhelmingly Catholic country, legally banned abortion. In 1983, a referendum affirming the ban through constitutional amendment passed by a two-thirds majority. However, the steady travel abroad of Irish women to have abortions, and a series of tragic cases involving the denial of abortion to women and in some cases, children, gave rise to public sentiment against the amendment. In 2016, the issue was turned over to the Citizen's Assembly. Sixty-four percent of the Assembly voted to legalize the termination of pregnancy within twelve weeks, and called for the government to put the matter to a referendum. Sixty-six percent of Irish voters agreed to the overturning of the ban (McKay 2019).

Besides the concrete legislative and policy results, perhaps the most hopeful outcome of such experiments is the seriousness with which participants approached their job and the respectfulness they showed to each other in deliberative polling and mini-publics. To get their jobs done, they strove in many cases to put their aversions to the positions of disagreeing others in a larger perspective. If nothing else, they put to shame the posturing and overheated rhetoric of politicians who address the issue (on deliberative polling, see Gessen 2019; on the Irish Citizen's Assembly, see McKay 2019; and podcast by Students at Central European University's School of Public Policy 2018).

24 Summary of Normative Moral Relativism

Normative moral relativism is not self-contradictory, but neither is it a complete ethic. It is based on metaethical relativism and the value of justifiability autonomy, but other values we hold, such as various rights we and other people have, may require actions incompatible with nonintervention and leaving others be. We may decide it is more important to act on these other values, or we may try to balance justifiability autonomy with these other values through modifying our way of acting on values such as rights. Ways of responding to the practice of female genital cutting may result from this sort of balancing. These ways also exemplify acting on the value of accommodation, which is a universal constraint on moralities.

Accommodation may also help in dealing with the extremely divisive issue of abortion. Part of the problem may be an absolutist conception of rights which leaves us less able to balance them against each other and other important considerations, and less able to accommodate others who think differently about the issue. The more fundamental problem may be our alienation from others who think differently. We have to be willing to engage with others in the spirit of getting a fuller picture of the complexity of their views, as we would want others to understand us. This spirit lies behind the best versions of moral relativism.

References

Abdulcadir, Jasmine, Botsikas, Diamides, Bolmont, Mylène et al. (2016). "Sexual Anatomy and Function in Women with and without Genital Mutilation: A Cross-Sectional Study," *The Journal of Sexual Medicine* 13(2), 226–237.

Adams, David Wallace (1995). *Education for Extinction: American Indians and the Boarding School Experience*. Lawrence: University Press of Kansas.

Ahmadu, Fuambai S. (2001). "Rites and Wrongs: An Insider/Outsider Reflects on Power and Excision," in Bettina Shell-Duncan and Yiva Herlund (eds.), *Female "Circumcision" in Africa: Culture, Controversy, and Change*, 283–312. Boulder, CO: Lynne Rienner.

Ahmadu, Fuambai S., and Shweder, Richard A. (2009). "Disputing the Myth of the Sexual Dysfunction of Circumcised Women: An Interview with Fuambai S. Ahmadu by Richard A. Shweder," *Anthropology Today* 25(6), 14–17.

Analects (2006–21). *Chinese Text Project*. https://ctext.org/analects.

Appiah, Kwame Anthony (2006). *Cosmopolitanism: Ethics in a World of Strangers*. New York: W. W. Norton.

Aristotle (2016). *Aristotle's Politics: Writings from the Complete Works – Politics, Economics, Constitution of Athens*, ed. Jonathan Barnes, trans. Benjamin Jowett, 1–225. Princeton, NJ: Princeton University Press.

Ayars, Alisabeth, and Nichols, Shaun (2020). "Rational Learners and Metaethics: Universalism, Relativism, and Evidence from Consensus," *Mind & Language* 35, 67–89.

Baier, Annette (1986). "Trust and Antitrust," *Ethics* 96(2), 231–260.

Berlin, Isaiah (2002). "Two Concepts of Liberty," in H. Hardy (ed.), *Liberty: Incorporating Four Essays on Liberty*. Oxford: Oxford University Press, 167–215.

Bloomfield, Paul (2009). "Review of *Natural Moralities: A Defense of Pluralistic Relativism*," *Mind*, 118(469), 225–230.

Boddy, Janice (2007). *Civilizing Women: British Crusades in Colonial Sudan*. Princeton, NJ: Princeton University Press.

Boddy, Janice (2016). "The Normal and the Aberrant in Female Genital Cutting: Shifting Paradigms," *HAU: Journal of Ethnographic Theory* 6(2), 41–69.

Boddy, Janice (2020). "Re-thinking the Zero Tolerance Approach to FGM/C: The Debate Around Female Genital Cosmetic Surgery," *Current Sexual Health Reports* 12(4), 302–313.

Brink, David (1989). *Moral Realism and the Foundation of Ethics*. Cambridge, UK: Cambridge University Press.

Bruce, Tricia C. (2020). "How Americans Understand Abortion: A Comprehensive Interview Study of Abortion Attitudes in the US," McGrath Institute for Church Life, University of Notre Dame, https://tinyurl.com/2xtjfz7j, accessed November 27, 2022.

Catania, Lucrezia, Abdulcadir, Omar, Puppo, Vincenzo et al. (2007). "Pleasure and Orgasm in Women with Female Genital Mutilation/Cutting (FGM/C)," *The Journal of Sexual Medicine* 4(6), 1666–1678.

Chan, Sin Yee (2000). "Gender and Relationship Roles in the *Analects* and the *Mencius*," *Asian Philosophy* 10(2), 115–131.

Chang, Iris (2003). *The Chinese in America*. New York: Viking Press.

Christensen, David (2007). "Epistemology of Disagreement: The Good News," *Philosophical Review* 116(2), 187–217.

Coulthard, Glen Sean (2014). *Red Skin, White Masks: Rejecting the Colonial Politics of Recognition*. Minneapolis: University of Minnesota Press.

Cowan, Sarah K., Bruce, Tricia C., Perry, Brea L. et al. (2022). "Discordant Benevolence: How and Why People Help Others in the Face of Conflicting Values," *Science Advances* 8, 1–16.

Cua, Antonio S. (1989). "The Status of Principles in Confucian Ethics," *Journal of Chinese Philosophy* 16(3–4), 273–296.

Curry, Oliver Scott, Mullins, Daniel Scott, and Whitehouse, Harvey (2019). "Is It Good to Cooperate? Testing the Theory of Morality-as-Cooperation in 60 Societies," *Current Anthropology* 60(1), 47–69.

de Waal, Frans B. M. (2008). "Putting the Altruism back into Altruism," *Annual Review of Psychology* 59(1), 279–300.

Dobbs v. Jackson Women's Health Organization (2022), 597 U.S.

Dreier, James (1990). "Internalism and Speaker Relativism," *Ethics* 101(1), 6–26.

Duivenbode, Rosie, and Padela, Aasim I. (2019). "The Problem of Female Genital Cutting: Bridging Secular and Islamic Bioethical Perspectives," *Perspectives in Biology and Medicine* 62(2), 273–300.

Dworkin, Ronald (1977). *Taking Rights Seriously*. Cambridge, MA: Harvard University Press.

Earp, Brian D. (2016). "Between Moral Relativism and Moral Hypocrisy: Reframing the Debate on 'FGM,'" *Kennedy Institute of Ethics Journal* 26(2), 105–144.

(2022). "Against Legalising Female 'Circumcision' of Minors: A Reply to 'The Prosecution of Dawoodi Bohra Women' by Richard Shweder," *Global Discourse* 12(1), 47–76.

Earp, Brian D., and Johnsdotter, Sara (2021). "Current Critiques of the WHO Policy on Female Genital Mutilation," *International Journal of Impotence Research* 33(2), 196–209.

Earp, Brian D., McLoughlin, Killian L., Monrad, Joshua T., Clark, Marsha S., and Crockett, Molly J. (2021). "How Social Relationships Shape Moral Wrongness Judgments," *Nature Communications* 12(1), 1–3.

Farrell, David M., Suiter, Jane, and Harris, Clodagh (2019). "Systematizing Constitutional Deliberation: The 2016–18 Citizens' Assembly in Ireland," *Irish Political Studies* 34(1), 113–123.

Fishkin, James (2009). *When the People Speak: Deliberative Democracy and Public Consultation*. New York: Oxford University Press.

Flack, Jessica C., and de Waal, Frans B. M. (2000). "Any Animal Whatever," *Journal of Consciousness Studies* 7(1–2), 1–29.

Fricker, Miranda (2007). *Epistemic Injustice: Power and the Ethics of Knowing*. Oxford: Oxford University Press.

Galbraith, Kate, and Price, Asher (2013). *The Great Texas Wind Rush: How George Bush, Ann Richards, and a Bunch of Tinkerers Helped the Oil and Gas State Win the Race to Wind Power*. Austin: University of Texas Press.

Gessen, Masha (2019). "What Happens When a Group of Strangers Spends a Day Debating Immigation?" *The New Yorker*, July 23, https://tinyurl.com/2p94wm2w, accessed November 27, 2022.

Gibbard, Allan (1992). *Wise Choices, Apt Feelings: A Theory of Normative Judgment*. Cambridge, MA: Harvard University Press.

Gil, Michael B. (2009). "Indeterminacy and Variability in Meta-Ethics," *Philosophical Studies* 145(2), 215–234.

Gillespie, Valerie (2020). "Let's Embrace Duke's Entire History," *Duke Magazine*, summer issue, https://tinyurl.com/stedvp9m, accessed November 27, 2022.

Gilligan, Carol (1982). *In a Different Voice: Psychological Theory and Women's Development*. Cambridge, MA: Harvard University Press.

Gintis, Herbert (2000). *Game Theory Evolving*. Princeton, NJ: Princeton University Press.

Goodwin, Geoffrey P., and Darley, John M. (2008). "The Psychology of Meta-Ethics: Exploring Objectivism," *Cognition* 106, 1339–1366.

Gowans, Christopher (2007). Review of *Natural Moralities: A Defense of Pluralistic Relativism*, *Notre Dame Philosophical Reviews*, April 14, https://tinyurl.com/5tzrc28h, accessed November 27, 2022.

Greene, Jamal (2021). *How Rights Went Wrong: Why Our Obsession with Rights Is Tearing America Apart*. Boston, MA: Houghton Mifflin Harcourt.

Gruenbaum, Ellen (2001). *Civilizing Women: British Crusades in Colonial Sudan*. Princeton, NJ: Princeton University Press.

Gruenbaum, Ellen, Earp, Bryan D., and Shweder, Richard A. (2022). "Reconsidering the Role of Patriarchy in Upholding Female Genital

Modifications," *International Journal of Impotence Research*, 1–10. www.nature.com/articles/s41443-022-00581-5, accessed November 27, 2022.

Hall, David L., and Ames, Roger T. (1987). *Thinking Through Confucius*. Albany: State University of New York Press.

Hamilton, William (1964). "The Genetical Evolution of Social Behavior," *Journal of Theoretical Biology* 7, 1–16.

Hanson, Eric, Gamez, Daniel P., and Manuel, Alexa (2020). "The Residential School System," *First Nations and Indigenous Studies UBC*, https://tinyurl.com/4y989byn, accessed November 27, 2022.

Harman, Gilbert (1975). "Moral Relativism Defended," *Philosophical Review* 84(1), 3–22.

(2000). *Explaining Value, and Other Essays in Moral Philosophy*. New York: Oxford University Press.

Harrison, Geoffrey (1976). "Relativism and Tolerance," *Ethics* 86(2), 122–135.

Heath, Malcolm (2008). "Aristotle on Natural Slavery," *Phronesis* 53, 243–270.

Held, Virginia (2006). *The Ethics of Care: Personal, Political, and Global*, 2nd edition. New York: Oxford University Press.

Hoffman, Martin L. (2000). *Empathy and Moral Development: Implications for Caring and Justice*. Cambridge, UK: Cambridge University Press.

Hollander, Michael and Sandelweiss, Martha A. (2022). "Princeton and Slavery: Holding the Center," *Princeton Alumni Weekly*, November 8, 2017, accessed online on June 19, 2022, https://paw.princeton.edu/issues/v118-n04-11082107.

Hourdequin, Marion (2021). "Environmental Ethics: The State of the Question," *Southern Journal of Philosophy* 59(3), 270–308.

Hourdequin, Marion and Wong. David B. (2005). "A Relational Approach to Environmental Ehics," *Journal of Chinese Philosophy* 32(1), 19–33.

Hrdy, Sarah Blaffer (2011). *Mothers and Others: The Evolutionary Origins of Mutual Understanding*. Cambridge, MA: Harvard University Press.

Kittay, Eva (1999). *Love's Labor: Essays on Women, Equality, and Dependency*. New York: Routledge.

Kölbel, M. (2003) "Faultless Disagreement," *Proceedings of the Aristotelian Society*, New Series, 104(1), 53–73.

(2013) "Relativism," *Philosophy Compass* 10(1), 38–51.

Kratz, Corinne A. (2002). "Circumcision Debates and Asylum Cases: Intersecting Arenas, Contested Values, and Tangled Webs," in Richard A. Shweder, Martha Minow, and Hazel Rose Markus (eds.), *Engaging Cultural*

Differences: The Multicultural Challenge in Liberal Democracies, 309–343. New York: Russell Sage Foundation.

Landemore, Hélène (2020). *Open Democracy: Reinventing Popular Rule for the Twenty-First Century*. Princeton, NJ: Princeton University Press.

LeDoux, Joseph E. (2002). *Synaptic Self: How Our Brains Become Who We Are*. New York: Viking.

Leonard, Lori (2000). "Interpreting Female Genital Cutting: Moving Beyond the Impasse," *Annual Review of Sex Research* 11(1), 158–190.

Li, Chenyang (1994). "The Confucian Concept of Jen and the Feminist Ethics of Care: A Comparative Study," *Hypatia*, 9(1), 70–89.

Lyons, Harriet D. (2007). "Genital Cutting: The Past and Present of a Polythetic Category," *Africa Today* 53(4), 3–17.

MacFarlane, J. (2007). "Relativism and Disagreement," *Philosophical Studies* 132, 17–31.

MacIntyre, Alasdair (1988). *Whose Justice? Which Rationality?* South Bend, IN: University of Notre Dame Press.

  (2007). *After Virtue*, 3rd edition. South Bend, IN: University of Notre Dame Press.

Mackie, John L. (1977). *Ethics: Inventing Right and Wrong*. London: Penguin Books.

Mandela, Nelson (2006). "The Ubuntu Experience," an interview of Nelson Mandela by Tim Modise, November 1, 2006. www.youtube.com/watch?v=ODQ4WiDsEBQ.

Markus, Hazel, and Kitayama, Shinobu (1991). "Culture and the Self: Implications for Cognition, Emotion, and Motivation," *Psychological Review* 98(2), 224–253.

McGrath, Sara (2010). "Moral Realism without Convergence," *Philosophical Topics* 38(2), 59–90.

McKay, Susan (2019). "A Jury of Peers: How Ireland Used a Citizen's Assembly to Solve Some of Its Toughest Problems," *Foreign Policy* 231, 5–7.

Mencius (*Mengzi* 2006–21). *Chinese Text Project*, https://ctext.org/mengzi, accessed November 23, 2022.

Metz, Thaddeus (2011). "Ubuntu as a Moral Theory and Human Rights in South Africa," *African Human Rights Law Journal* 11(2), 532–559.

Millett, Paul (2007). "Aristotle and Slavery in Athens," *Greece & Rome* 54(2), 178–209.

Möeller, Kai (2012). "Proportionality: Challenging the Critics," *International Journal of Constitutional Law* 10(3), 709–731.

Moody-Adams, Michele (1997). *Fieldwork in Familiar Places: Morality, Culture, & Philosophy*. Cambridge, MA: Harvard University Press.

Morel, Mary Kay (1997). "Captain Pratt's School," *American History* 32(2), 26–32, 62–64.

Murdock, Esme (2020). "Troubling Ecological Citizenship: Expanding Our Minds and Hearts to See the More-Than-Human World as Our Relations," *Minding Nature* 13(2), 36–41.

 (2022). "Indigenous Governance Now: Settler Colonial Injustice Is Not Historically Past," *Critical Review of International Social and Political Philosophy* 25(3), 411–426.

Njambi, Wairimŭ Ngaruiya (2004). "Dualisms and Female Bodies in Representations of African Female Circumcision: A Feminist Critique," *Feminist Theory* 5(3), 281–303.

 (2011). "Irua Ria Atumia and Anticolonial Struggles among the Gĩkũyũ of Kenya: A Counternarrative on 'Female Genital Mutilation,'" in Oyèrónkẹ́ Oyěwùmí (ed.), *Gender Epistemologies in Africa: Gendering Traditions, Spaces, Social Institutions, and Identities*, 179–197. New York: Palgrave Macmillan.

Noddings, Nel (1984). *Caring: A Feminine Approach to Ethics and Moral Education*. Berkeley: University of California Press.

Nussbaum, Martha (2001). *Upheavals of Thought*. Cambridge, UK: Cambridge University Press.

Oba, Abdulmumini A. (2008). "Female Circumcision as Female Genital Mutilation: Human Rights or Cultural Imperialism?" *Global Jurist* 8(3). doi: 10.2202/1934-2640.1286/html

Okasha, Samir (2020). "Biological Altruism," in Edward N. Zalta (ed.), *The Stanford Encyclopedia of Philosophy* (Summer 2020 Edition), https://stanford.io/3U5gOEQ, accessed November 23, 2022.

Olinder, Ragnar Francén (2012). "Moral and Metaethical Pluralism: Unity in Variation," *The Southern Journal of Philosophy* 50(4), 583–601.

Ostrom, Carol M. 1996. "Harborview Debates Issue of Circumcision of Muslim Girls." *The Seattle Times*, September 13, 1996, www.bit.ly/3id1AAq, accessed November 27, 2022.

Pande, Raksha (2021). "Young British Indians Are Embracing Marriage – Just Not in the Traditional Sense," April 29, 2021, *The Conversation*, www.bit.ly/3ARqex4, accessed November 27, 2022.

Park, John J. (2022). *The Psychological Basis of Moral Judgments: Philosophical and Empirical Approaches to Moral Relativism*. New York: Routledge.

Planned Parenthood v. *Casey* (1992). 505 U.S. 833.

Prinz, Jesse J. (2007). *The Emotional Construction of Morals* Oxford: Oxford University Press.

Public Policy Advisory Network on Female Genital Surgeries in Africa. (2012). "Seven Things to Know about Female Genital Surgeries in Africa," *Hastings Center Report* 42(6), 19–27.

Quinn, Naomi (2005). "Universals of Child Rearing," *Anthropological Theory* 5, 477–516.

R. v. Morgentaler (1988). https://scc-csc.lexum.com/scc-csc/scc-csc/en/item/288/index.do, accessed July 23, 2022.

Rakove, Jack (2009). *The Annotated US Constitution and Declaration of Independence*. Cambridge, MA: Belknap Press of Harvard University Press.

Railton, Peter (1989). " Railton, "Naturalism and Prescriptivity," *Social Philosophy and Policy* 7, 151–174.

Richardson, Heather Cox (2020). *How the South Won the Civil War*. New York: Oxford University Press.

Richardson, James D. (2004). *A Compilation of the Messages and Papers of the Presidents Section 1 (of 2) of Volume 3: Andrew Jackson (Second Term)*. Project Gutenberg EBook. http://gutenberg.readingroo.ms/1/1/2/0/11202/11202.txt.

Richerson, Peter J., and Boyd, Robert (2005). *Not By Genes Alone*. Chicago, IL: University of Chicago Press.

Richerson, Peter J., Boyd, Robert, and Henrich, Joseph (2003). "Cultural Evolution of Human Cooperation," in P. Hammerstein (ed.), *Genetic and Cultural Evolution of Cooperation: A Dahlem Conference Workshop*. Cambridge: MA: MIT Press.

Roe v. Wade (1973). 410 U.S. 113.

Rosenlee, Li-Hsiang Lisa (2014). "Why Care? A Feminist Re-appropriation of Confucian *Xiao*," in A. Olberding (ed.), *Dao Companion to the Analects*, 311–334. Dordrecht: Springer.

Rovane, Carol (2013). *The Metaphysics and Ethics of Relativism*. Cambridge, MA: Harvard University Press.

Ruddick, Sara (1989). "Maternal Thinking," in A. Trebilcot (ed.), *Mothering: Essays in Feminist Theory*, 213–230. Totowa, NJ: Rowman and Allanheld.

Sandel, Michael (1998). *Liberalism and the Limits of Justice*, 2nd edition. New York: Cambridge University Press.

Sarkissian, Hagop (2017). "Folk Platitudes as the Explananda of Philosophical Metaethics: Are They Accurate? And Do They Help or Hinder Inquiry?" *Journal of the Indian Council of Philosophical Research* 34, 565–575.

Scanlon, Thomas M. (1998). *What We Owe to Each Other*. Cambridge, MA: Harvard University Press.

Shafer-Landau, Russ (1994). "Ethical Disagreement, Ethical Objectivism, and Moral Indeterminacy," *Philosophy and Phenomenological Research* 54(2), 331–344.

(1995). "Vagueness, Borderline Cases and Moral Realism," *American Philosophical Quarterly* 32(1), 83–96.

(2003). *Moral Realism: A Defense.* New York: Oxford University Press.

Shell-Duncan, Bettina, and Hernlund, Ylva (2000). "Female 'Circumcision' in Africa: Dimensions of the Practice and Debates," in Bettina Shell-Duncan and Ylva Herlund (eds.), *Female "Circumcision" in Africa: Culture, Controversy, and Change,* 1–40. Boulder, CO: Lynne Rienner Publishers.

Shweder, Richard A. (2003). "What about Female Genital Mutilation?," in *Why Do Men Barbecue? Recipes for Cultural Psychology,* 168–216. Cambridge, MA: Harvard University Press.

(2022). "The Prosecution of Dawoodi Bohra Women: Some Reasonable Doubts," *Global Discourse* 12(1), 9–27.

Smith, Michael (1994). *The Moral Problem.* Oxford: Blackwell Publishing.

Sober, Elliot, and Wilson, David S. (1998). *Unto Others: The Evolution and Psychology of Unselfish Behavior.* Cambridge, MA: Harvard University Press.

Sophocles (1984). *The Three Theban Plays: Antigone; Oedipus the King; Oedipus at Colonus,* trans. Robert Fagles. New York: Penguin Books.

Srvluga, Susan (2015). "Former Ole Miss Student Sentenced to Six Months for Putting Noose Around Statue." *Washington Post,* September 17, 2015, www.bit.ly/3VfaVGG, accessed November 27, 2022.

Street, Sharon (2006). "A Darwinian Dilemma for Realist Theories of Value," *Philosophical Studies* 127, 109–166.

Students at Central European University's School of Public Policy (2018). *Tend It Like a Garden: A Podcast on the Irish Citizens' Assembly.* www.bit.ly/3u4nskb, accessed November 27, 2022.

Tajfel, Henri (1970). "Experiments in Intergroup Discrimination," *Scientific American* 223, 96–102.

Tajfel, Henri Billig, M. G. Bundy, R. P., and Flament, Claude (1971). "Social Categorization and Intergroup Behaviour," *European Journal of Social Psychology* 1, 149–178.

Tajfel, Henri, and Turner, J. (1979). "An Integrative Theory of Intergroup Conflict," in W. G. Austin and S. Worchel (eds.), *The Social Psychology of Intergroup Relations,* 33–47. Monterey, CA: Brooks/Cole.

Taylor, Charles (1985). *Philosophy and the Human Sciences: Philosophical Papers 2.* Cambridge, UK: Cambridge University Press.

(1989). *Sources of the Self: The Making of the Modern Identity*. Cambridge, UK: Cambridge University Press.

Thomas, Lynn M. (1996). "'Ngaitana (I Will Circumcise Myself)': The Gender and Generational Politics of the 1956 Ban on Clitoridectomy in Meru, Kenya," *Gender and History* 8(3), 338–363.

Tomasello, Michael (2019). *Becoming Human: A Theory of Ontogeny*. Cambridge, MA: Belknap Press of Harvard University Press.

Triandis, Harry C. (1995). *Individualism and Collectivism*. Boulder, CO: Westview Press.

Trivers, Robert (1971). "The Evolution of Reciprocal Altruism," *Quarterly Review of Biology* 46(1), 35–57.

Tronto, Joan (1993). *Moral Boundaries: A Political Argument for an Ethic of Care*. New York: Routledge.

Velleman, David (2013). *Foundations for Moral Relativism*. Cambridge, UK: Open Book Publishers.

Walker, Margaret Urban (2007). *Moral Understandings: A Feminist Study in Ethics*, 2nd edition. New York: Oxford University Press.

Wang, Peter (1986). *A Great Wall* [film]. W&S Productions & Nanhai Film Co.

Whyte, Kyle P. (2018). "What Do Indigenous Knowledges Do for Indigenous Peoples?" in Melissa K. Nelson and Dan Shilling (eds.), *Traditional Ecological Knowledge*, 57–81. Cambridge, UK: Cambridge University Press.

Williams, Bernard (1981). "The Truth in Relativism," in *Moral Luck*, 132–143. Cambridge, UK: Cambridge University Press.

Wong, David B. (1984). *Moral Relativity*. Berkeley, CA: University of California Press.

(2006). *Natural Moralities: A Defense of Pluralistic Relativism*. New York: Oxford University Press.

(2011). "Relativist Explanations of Interpersonal and Group Disagreement," in Steven D. Hales (ed.), *A Companion to Relativism*, 411–430. Malden, MA: Wiley-Blackwell.

(2014). "David Wong's Responses to Critics," in Yang Xiao and Yong Hong (eds.), *Moral Relativism and Chinese Philosophy*, 181–274. Albany: State University of New York Press.

(2015a). "Early Confucian Philosophy and the Development of Compassion," *Dao* 14(2), 157–194.

(2015b). "Growing Virtue: The Theory and Science of Developing Compassion from a Mencian Perspective," in Brian Bruya (ed.), *The Philosophical Challenge from China*, 23–56. Cambridge, MA: MIT Press.

(2019a). "Relativism and Pluralism in Moral Epistemology," in Aaron Zimmerman, Karen Jones, Mark Timmons (eds.), *The Routledge Handbook of Moral Epistemology*, 316–328. New York: Routledge.

(2019b). "Morality, Definition of," in Hugh LaFollette (ed.), *International Encyclopedia of Ethics*, 4488–4499. Hoboken, NJ: John Wiley & Sons.

World Health Organization (2008). "Eliminating Female Genital Mutilation: An Interagency Statement," www.unfpa.org/sites/default/files/pub-pdf/eliminating_fgm.pdf, accessed July 19, 2022.

World Population Review (2022) "Abortion Laws by State 2022," https://tinyurl.com/4mmpnzyw, accessed November 27, 2022.

Wright, Jennifer C., Grandjean, Piper T., and McWhite, Cullen B. (2013). "The Meta-ethical Grounding of Our Moral Beliefs: Evidence for Meta-ethical Pluralism," *Philosophical Psychology* 26(3), 336–361.

Xiao Jing (*Classic of Filial Piety*) (2006–21). *Chinese Text Project.* https://ctext.org/xiao-jing, accessed November 23, 2022.

Xunzi (2006–21). *Chinese Text Project.* https://ctext.org/xunzi, accessed November 23, 2022.

Yoder, P. Stanley, Wang, Shanxiao, and Johansen, Elise (2013). "Estimates of Female Genital Mutilation/Cutting in 27 African Countries and Yemen," *Studies in Family Planning* 44(2), 189–204.

Acknowledgments

I wish to thank Dale E. Miller, Ben Eggleston, and an anonymous reviewer for their many helpful comments.

For Liana and Z

Ethics

Ben Eggleston
University of Kansas

Ben Eggleston is a professor of philosophy at the University of Kansas. He is the editor of John Stuart Mill, *Utilitarianism: With Related Remarks from Mill's Other Writings* (Hackett, 2017) and a co-editor of *Moral Theory and Climate Change: Ethical Perspectives on a Warming Planet* (Routledge, 2020), *The Cambridge Companion to Utilitarianism* (Cambridge, 2014), and *John Stuart Mill and the Art of Life* (Oxford, 2011). He is also the author of numerous articles and book chapters on various topics in ethics.

Dale E. Miller
Old Dominion University, Virginia

Dale E. Miller is a professor of philosophy at Old Dominion University. He is the author of *John Stuart Mill: Moral, Social and Political Thought* (Polity, 2010) and a co-editor of *Moral Theory and Climate Change: Ethical Perspectives on a Warming Planet* (Routledge, 2020), *A Companion to Mill* (Blackwell, 2017), *The Cambridge Companion to Utilitarianism* (Cambridge, 2014), *John Stuart Mill and the Art of Life* (Oxford, 2011), and *Morality, Rules, and Consequences: A Critical Reader* (Edinburgh, 2000). He is also the editor-in-chief of *Utilitas*, and the author of numerous articles and book chapters on various topics in ethics broadly construed.

About the Series

This Elements series provides an extensive overview of major figures, theories, and concepts in the field of ethics. Each entry in the series acquaints students with the main aspects of its topic while articulating the author's distinctive viewpoint in a manner that will interest researchers.

Cambridge Elements ≡

Ethics

A full series listing is available at www.cambridge.org/EETH